W9-BEX-646

HELL

BY GREGG WEAR

Unless otherwise indicated, all Scripture quotations are taken from the *King James Version* of the Bible.

HELL

Copyright 2000 by Gregg Wear
P.O. Box 1193
Sedalia, MO 65302

ISBN # 0-9671368-4-9

Printed in the United States of America. All rights reserved under International Copyright Law. Contents and/or cover may not be reproduced in whole or in part in any form without the express written consent of the Publisher.

HELL
A Spiritual Nightmare
From Which There
Is No Waking

OTHER BOOKS BY GREGG WEAR

UNTANGLING THE HEALING CRISIS

This 206 page book answers the many questions people ask about divine healing. Divine healing is unmistakably the will of God for all, but what about Job? Paul's thorn in the flesh? Timothy's weak stomach? The man born blind in John 9? This is written in such a way to help the reader understand why God wants them to be healed and *how* healing can be received.

FAITH — THE SUPERNATURAL CONNECTION

This 200 page book explains how to make the supernatural connection with God in prayer. Prayer and faith are not difficult, they simply have to be learned. The reason faith has seemed difficult for some is because of a lack of understanding from the Bible on *how* to believe and *how* to get strong faith. This book makes faith easy to grasp.

BEATING THE BLAME GAME

This 200 page book proves from the Bible that God is not responsible for the sorrow and tragedy in the world. Much confusion exists in the Body of Christ on the subject of suffering, tests, and trials. The good news is, God is not responsible for disease, poverty, and tragedy. This book will help the reader to grasp the goodness of God and how to rise above the circumstances of life.

(Books continued next page)

Other Books by Gregg Wear, continued

PIECING TOGETHER THE
PROSPERITY PUZZLE

This 201 page book proves from the Bible that God wants His children to prosper financially. Assuming the Christian tithes and gives offerings then *how* does God bring prosperity to pass in his life. This book answers this question, as well as the ultimate purpose for financial prosperity. Like all other truths in the Bible, prosperity is not difficult it just has to be learned.

The price of each book is $10.00, plus $2.00 for shipping and handling. To order, write:

Gregg Wear Ministries
P.O. Box 1193
Sedalia, MO 65302

TABLE OF CONTENTS

- Table of Contents Continued Next Page

TABLE OF CONTENTS, continued

PREFACE

There are a number of Hebrew and Greek words translated hell in the Old and New Testaments. These will be looked at in more detail in chapter 8. Until closer examination is needed, I will use the general term "hell" in describing the spiritual underworld where the unredeemed dead presently abide.

Technically speaking, in the New Testament concerning mankind, hell is derived from two Greek words, *hades* and *Gehenna*. *Gehenna* is the ultimate destination for the unredeemed. It is also called the lake of fire in Revelation 20:14. This judgment will take place at what is called the great white throne judgment (Revelation 20:11-12). At that point, death and *hades* will be cast into the lake of fire.

Until that day takes place, the unredeemed, at physical death, go to *hades*. *Hades* simply means, *"the abode or dwelling place of the dead."* Before Christ's resurrection, *both* the righteous and unrighteous went to *hades*. *Hades* was divided into two sections — 1) paradise, where there was comfort, and 2) hell, where there was and is torment. Obviously, the righteous went to paradise, and the unrighteous went to hell.

At Christ's resurrection, paradise was removed from *hades* and taken to heaven. Now when the redeemed physically die, they go *up* to paradise. The unredeemed still go down into *hades*, into the hell section, where they are awaiting their final judgment, the lake of fire.

9

Some people consider teaching on hell too frightening and uncomfortable to devote pulpit time to. However, the fact that Jesus warned the people listening to him about hell on varied occasions and at different locations warrants that we study the subject of hell. If hell seems to be frightening now on earth, what about those presently in hell? Frightening is too tame of a word for them in their predicament. The fact is, if the Bible discusses hell, it merits our attention and study.

HELL

SECTION 1

CHRIST'S REVELATION OF HELL

Introduction

The very word "hell" brings disgust to the mind. It conjures thoughts of loathing, despising, and hating. For a person to tell another, *"Go to hell,"* means to wish the absolute worst upon the other. That any good in their life would be completely obliterated by all bad. It is the ultimate expression of hatred and ill-will.

The word "hell" also brings terror to the mind. It brings thoughts of a place so utterly horrific, so fearful, that the worst nightmare imaginable doesn't begin to describe it. To realize that there is an actual place called hell, and that people are already in torment there with more yet to go, causes one to wonder just how it could be avoided. Without a doubt, hell is the zenith of sorrow, pain, and misery.

Yet what is hell? What is in it? Where is it? Who was it made for? What takes place in it? Why is it? Why do people go there? The Bible has much to say about it and, in one instance, pulls back the veil to let us see what is on the other side of death (Luke 16:19-31).

Sadly, each and every day, multiplied thousands die and go to hell. Five minutes after they have taken their last breath they quickly realize there was much more to life than eating, drinking, and being merry. They had made preparation for their retirement, their stock portfolio looked good, their last will and testament saw to their children benefitting from their assets and estate, yet little preparation had been made with eternity in mind. It's amazing how people can see to the minutest detail in earthly matters, yet overlook the more important spiritual matters.

Jesus told of such a man in his day:

The ground of a certain rich man brought forth plentifully: And he thought within himself, saying, What shall I do, because I have no room where to bestow my fruits? And he said, This will I do: I will pull down my barns, and build greater; and there will I bestow all my fruits and my goods. And I will say to my soul, Soul, thou hast much goods laid up for many years; take thine ease, eat, drink, and be merry.

But God said unto him, Thou fool, this night thy soul shall be required of thee: then whose shall those things be, which thou hast provided? So is he that layeth up treasure for himself, and is not rich toward God.

- Luke 12:16-21

This rich farmer knew how to maximize the potential of his land. He obviously had the ability to stabilize through times of drought and leaner years. In better times and bumper crop years, he knew how to take advantage of his storehouses and save. In fact, his farming had been so successful he was ready to enlarge his enterprise and, at the same time, relax and enjoy the fruits of his labors.

According to the world's standards, this farmer was a success. He was rich, powerful, and exercised much influence on others in his community. The problem was, though, irrespective of the world's opinion, God considered this man to be a fool. Why? *Because he thought only for today with little regard for eternity.*

Obviously, then, the decisions we make based on eternal consequences are more important than decisions based on temporal consequences. What good is it if we end up being the most powerful person on earth politically or financially yet end up going to hell? Those already in hell wish they would have traded everything on earth for a right relationship with God. But, alas, for them it's now too late. Like this farmer, they chose the fool's gold over the real gold, and they're weeping bitter tears over their stupid, fateful decision.

It's important to realize as we study the subject of hell

that, no matter how graphically we try to picture hell in our mind's eye, in actuality, hell is far worse. The natural mind can't comprehend spiritual suffering. On earth our lives, by a far lesser degree, are a combination of both heaven and hell. In other words, on earth there is some joy mixed with some depression, and some pleasure mixed with some pain. However, in heaven there is pure pleasure, and in hell pure pain. It's difficult to imagine a place without the least bit of pleasure and joy, or a place without the least bit of depression and pain. Just as it is impossible to fully comprehend the magnificent wonders of what heaven will be like, it is likewise impossible to fully comprehend the depths of suffering and despair of what hell will be like.

Many striking descriptions of *hades* and *Gehenna* are depicted in the scriptures. Here are a sample few:

unquenchable fire	**Matthew 3:10, 12**
hell fire	**Matthew 5:22, 18:9,**
	Mark 9:43-49
cast into the fire	**Matthew 7:19**
furnace of fire	**Matthew 13:40-50**
cast into everlasting fire	**Matthew 18:8, 25:41,**
	46
fire that shall never	
be quenched	**Mark 9:43-49,**
	Luke 3:17
tormented in this flame	**Luke 16:24**
vengeance of eternal fire	**Jude 6,7**
tormented with fire and	
brimstone	**Revelation 19:20,**
	21:8

14

Little imagination is needed to picture the intolerable pain associated with fire. Whether you look at this fire metaphorically or literally, the truth is, the suffering of hell must be unimaginable. Hell is a place of fear and dread, to say the least. A place to be avoided at any and all cost. For people to live their lives without any regard for heaven or hell, concentrating only on their 70 or 80 years of earthly life, is stupidity of the highest rank.

Jesus even went so far as to tell us to remove anything that might take us to hell and the eventual lake of fire. Notice:

And if thy right eye offend thee, pluck it out, and cast it from thee: for it is profitable for thee that one of thy members should perish, and not that thy whole body should be cast into hell. And if thy right hand offend thee, cut it off, and cast it from thee: for it is profitable for thee that one of thy members should perish, and not that thy whole body should be cast into hell.

- Matthew 5:29-30

Of course, no one has to pluck out their eye or cut off their hand to avoid hell. Nevertheless, if someone's eye or hand would be instrumental in keeping them from living for God and, ultimately, being responsible for them going to hell, in Jesus' mind, it would easily be worth losing to avoid hell. Hell is just too bad and heaven is just too good for an eye or hand to lead someone to make a foolish decision. The point is, *nothing is more important in God's thinking than for people to avoid going to hell.*

It's interesting how many people and churches avoid

15

even talking about hell. Granted, it's not a pleasant subject. However, it is a very important subject. I didn't particularly enjoy talking to my young children about strangers, in warning them about taking candy from them or getting in their cars. I was concerned I would leave them with an unhealthy fear of all people, not just the bad. But because their safety and welfare meant everything to me, I had to attempt to inform them on a matter that was very important. It wasn't easy and certainly wasn't pleasant, and I may have overdone it in making my point, but it was something that had to be said.

Likewise, hell, as gruesome as it may be, is a subject that must be talked about periodically. Though not pleasant, it is a necessity for people to hear about this detestable place so that they can make the correct decision to avoid going there. It must also be admitted that any information about hell is interesting, if not eerily fascinating. Fortunately, the scriptures are not silent about the spiritual underworld. Much has been revealed in both the Old and New testaments.

The best news is, of course, no one has to go to hell. Jesus plainly said, *"I go to prepare a place for you. If it was not so, I would have told you"* (John 14:2). The fact is, there are many, many mansions reserved for those who choose to believe in Jesus (John 14:2). Hell can be avoided, and heaven can be gained with a short, basic prayer spoken in simple faith. Though there are multiplied millions in hell right now, not one of them had to go there. God wasn't willing that any of them should have perished. Make sure you don't make the same mistake.

CHAPTER
1

The Rich Man
And Lazarus

There was a certain rich man, which was clothed in purple and fine linen, and fared sumptuously every day: And there was a certain beggar named Lazarus, which was laid at his gate, full of sores, And desiring to be fed with the crumbs which fell from the rich man's table: moreover the dogs came and licked his sores.

And it came to pass, that the beggar died, and was carried by the angels into Abraham's bosom: the rich man also died, and was buried: And in hell he lift up his eyes, being in torments, and seeth Abraham afar off, and Lazarus in his bosom.

And he cried and said, Father Abraham, have mercy on me, and send Lazarus, that he may dip the tip of his finger in water, and cool my tongue; for I am tormented in this flame. But Abraham said, Son, remember that thou in thy lifetime receivedst thy good things, and likewise Lazarus evil things: but now he is comforted, and thou art tormented. And beside all this, between us and you there is a great gulf fixed: so that they which would pass from hence to you cannot; neither can they pass to us, that would come from thence.

Then he said, I pray thee therefore, father, that thou wouldest send him to my father's house: For I have five brethren; that he may testify unto them, lest they also come into this place of torment. Abraham saith unto him, They have Moses and the prophets; let them hear them.

And he said, Nay, father Abraham: but if one went unto them from the dead, they will repent. And he said unto him, If they hear not Moses and the prophets, neither will they be persuaded, though one rose from the dead.

Luke 16:19-31

That the dead are conscious after death in either comfort or torment is revealed in no uncertain terms by the very words of our Lord Jesus Christ. Jesus pulled back the veil of the afterlife to let us peer across the gulf of death to see what happens to the spirit and soul after it leaves the body at physical death. There is no need to guess about what happens to people when they die. According to Jesus, they go to either one of two places. Not three. Not four. Only *two* places. After death they are either in torment or in comfort.

Jesus tells us about two individuals who lived on the earth at one time. One individual lived only for this world without regard to spiritual matters, the other looked to God and chose to believe that God would care for him when his physical life drew to a close. Lazarus, whose very name means *"God hath helped,"* obviously had faith in the God of Abraham, Isaac, and Jacob. The rich man, who evidently was acquainted with repentance (Luke 16:30), chose to disregard anything spiritual and pursued a course of self-will.

Some have considered this account to be a parable. This is incorrect. Never, in any of the parables that Jesus told, did He use actual names. Here Jesus specifically tells us that one of the individuals in the narrative was named Lazarus. Further, a parable is a story designed to teach a moral or religious principle by suggesting a parallel. Certainly there are religious principles in this account to be gleaned, but specifically, Jesus here is not suggesting a parallel, he is giving us a *direct statement*, or more accurately, a *direct revelation* of the spirit world. Also, in my thinking, if Jesus plainly stated, "There was a *certain* rich man" (Luke 16:19). it would be impossible for me not to believe there was a certain rich man. Thus, in this narrative are two individuals, a certain rich man and Lazarus.

Realize this also, the rich man didn't go to hell because he was rich, and the beggar named Lazarus didn't go to paradise because he was poor. Whether we are rich or poor has no bearing on where our spirits go after death. Hell has many, many poor people in it, and paradise has many, many rich people in it. In fact, Abraham, for whom many refer to paradise as Abraham's bosom was, most likely, far, far richer than this rich man in hell. As far as that goes, paradise was full of many rich people — Isaac, Jacob, Joseph, David, Hezekiah, Uzziah, and Job, to name just a few. Sadly, though, this rich man chose to trust in his riches over the God of heaven and lived only for the comfort of this natural world.

The fact that he called Abraham, "*Father* Abraham," indicates this rich man was of Jewish descent. Yet even though his national heritage believed in the God of Abraham, Isaac, and Jacob, his lineage wasn't enough to keep *him* out of hell. It must have seemed odd to have been one of the chosen people by birth yet end up in hell. This gives us some insight into salvation under the Old Covenant. Evidently repentance was necessary then as now. Just because one was born a Jew didn't mean that heaven was a certainty. They, too, had to be persuaded to believe (Luke 16:31).

The purpose for Jesus giving us this narrative is to eliminate any confusion about how people are existing in the next life. In fact, Jesus settles the issue once and for all that physical death is not the cessation of existence. Some want to believe that when people die they are dead like a dead dog or cat. Nothing could be further from the truth. Jesus revealed that man is more than beast. Man is eternal, and consciousness survives death.

Exactly what this rich man believed is not known. He either didn't believe in God, or perhaps though he did, chose not to let that knowledge influence the way he lived. In either case, he wasn't prepared when death came knocking at his door. It's strange how people choose to ignore that which is unpleasant. Because death is not a pleasant subject most tend to divert their thinking to lighter subjects, as if that will cause death to go elsewhere. Yet a brief look at the human life span should make us realize that, sooner or later, death will come to all of us. No one is exempt, and ignoring death isn't the way to deal with it. Faith in the Lord Jesus Christ is the only sane way to deal with death.

Anyway, this rich man died. As he quickly learned, death wasn't the cessation of existence, only the *transference* of existence. When he stepped outside of his dead body it must have been an awful terror to realize he was entering a sphere of existence for which he had made no preparation. Business acumen was of no value where he was headed. It's difficult to imagine the absolute fear that must have permeated his entire being. Most likely, he was in a state of shock, *"This can't be happening to me. This must be a nightmare from which I've got to wake any moment. This can't actually be what I think it is. Certainly not me. I've got to somehow get back into my body. I need more time."*

But time for him had run out. He started gravitating away from his dead body down into the lower regions of the earth. The farther he descended the darker it got. Soon he entered through the gates of hell to begin his spiritual confinement away from all that is holy and righteous. In hell he lift up his eyes being in torment (Luke 16: 23).

At this point, it might be of interest to go back to the surface of the earth. The moment he died his friends and loved ones no doubt grieved over his passing. Of course, they didn't realize he was just as much conscious now as he was while still in the body. They also probably didn't realize that at that very moment while they were hugging his lifeless body he was just beginning his duration in hell. To them his life was now over and it was time to plan the funeral.

21

Hell

Being a man of wealth we can surmise that his funeral was lavish — the most beautiful array of flowers, the finest burial perfumes in the embalming, and a noted sepulcher. No doubt many good words were conferred upon him by loved ones, friends, and those of similar standing in the community. A well-known rabbi delivered the eulogy, and the procession made its way to the sepulcher. Once the body was placed in the sarcophagus and the final words were spoken, the crowd slowly made its way back to town.

Surely the funeral was the talk of the community for several days. Friends and family rehearsed his kind deeds and benefactions. His five brothers divided his estate adding to their own security and comfort. And, occasionally, people visited the tomb to pay their respects, but over time as life continued to grind, this rich man became a distant memory to those who lived on. Of course, those who survived his death eventually passed away as well, and those in later generations recognized his name only as a distant relative on the family tree.

While life continued to grind its unending wheel as each generation came and went, this rich man continued to exist in torment in hell. His riches and prominence long forgotten, he most likely wished over and over that he had paid more attention to the rabbi as he had taught in the temple. But no, he knew he had only entertained information that would add to the creature comforts of his life. Anything spiritual was considered mundane and boring. The temple life wasn't nearly as exciting as the possibilities of tearing down his barns to build bigger barns. The merging of God and business didn't figure into any of his plans. Yet now, lost in the never ceasing torment of spiritual suffering, he regretted a thousand times over the reckless decisions he had made while on earth.

On earth most people abandon themselves to pleasure, comfort, and temporal security. He, too, thought only of such things. Yet in hell he realized he had wasted his 70 or 80 year probation, for that is basically what life on earth is, on what had then seemed important and exciting for what was now known as foolish and selfish. While Lazarus laid at his gate full of sores and half starved, he was selfishly indulging in excess and pride. Now he wished he wouldn't have ignored the hapless victims of society who were less fortunate than he — the feeble minded, the poor, and the sick.

The other individual in this narrative, Lazarus, was a beggar. How he got in this condition we don't know. Perhaps he was incapable of working through either disease or physical handicap. Since he *laid* at the rich man's gate, it seems logical to assume that he was unable to walk. Whatever the case, he was certainly in bad physical shape as he was full of sores. He was at the rich man's gate, not because he had been invited, but because of hunger, desperation, and great need. Nevertheless, in spite of his deteriorated physical condition, spiritually speaking, he believed in the one true God of his Jewish ancestors. His faith was not of this world, but of the next. When death came, he was ready.

And it came to pass, that the beggar died, and was carried by the angels into Abraham's bosom:
- Luke 16:22

We learn from this that when believers die, angels escort them to paradise. Believers don't leave this world alone, they're accompanied by God's angelic ministering spirits. Death, for a believer, is not a sad experience. To the unknowledgeable loved ones left behind it may be, but to the one who has departed, it's a time of exhilaration, joy, and happy reunion.

When Lazarus stepped outside of his lifeless body the angels were waiting to receive his spirit, and lovingly cared for him as they carried him into Abraham's bosom. Now he wasn't full of sores and no longer desiring crumbs. Dressed in the best of apparel, no longer in want of any kind, he was getting ready to experience unparalleled bliss.

On earth he may not have even had a funeral, perhaps just a pauper's burial in a mass grave. Society may not have even noticed he was gone. But many years later, unknown to the succeeding generations after him, he was best friends with Abraham, the prophets, and all others who had looked forward to the coming of the messiah. However many the years he lived on earth they were but a brief blip on the scale of the eternity. Nothing to look back to, everything to look forward to.

We see that life on earth is ridiculously short. One experienced great wealth, the other tremendous poverty. Sadly, all that most people can think about is how they'll live for this day with little regard for their eternal future. If they do think about God, it's a decision they purposely put off until they're old and retired. As far as they're concerned, there is too much fun to enjoy today. God can wait. Now is the time to eat, drink, and be merry.

Most people live as if they're going to live for 10,000 years, not realizing that eternity is only one heartbeat away. Without God, regardless of our age, we have no assurance we'll be alive 24 hours from now. Freak accidents, automobile accidents, allergic reactions, physical complications, or something as simple as choking on food at dinner time, can bring unexpected and sudden death. Most think they'll have time to prepare for death, but life on earth carries no such guarantee. It's imperative to make a decision for Christ while we're in our right mind, because when death unexpectedly happens, all our plans are immediately discarded to the wayside.

Lazarus had made the right decision, the rich man the wrong decision. The rich man must still be bitterly rehearsing in his mind the wasted opportunities. Lazarus must still be rejoicing over his faith while on earth. With eternity in front of both of them, one dreads what it holds, the other anticipates what it holds. One fears his present and future, the other is rejoicing over his present and future. Avoiding hell and gaining heaven is only a simple prayer away. Sadly, too many never pray that prayer.

CHAPTER 2

The Rich Man In Hell

And in hell he lift up his eyes, being in torments...
- Luke 16:23

It states that this rich man died and was buried. To most people that marked the end of this man's existence. However, it was really only the beginning, or more accurately, a *continuation*. Life on earth is the initial start and, in comparison to multiplied billions of years, so very short. It's interesting how some think that, regardless of how a life was lived on earth, upon death they become saints. To hear what is said at many funerals you would think that the one in the casket, even if he was a known atheist or agnostic, had become something of a spiritual person. As a result of such sermons at funerals many have a false security about their own eternal welfare. The truth is, however, if we live in sin, we die in sin:

I said therefore unto you, that ye shall die in your sins: for if ye believe not that I am he, ye shall die in your sins.

- John 8:24

27

Upon death, this rich man found that there was no change made in his nature. What he was 5 minutes before death he was still 5 minutes after death. If he had faintly hoped that he would somehow enter paradise he was sadly disappointed. His nature wouldn't allow such an entrance:

He that is unjust, let him be unjust still: and he which is filthy, let him be filthy still: and he that is righteous, let him be righteous still: and he that is holy, let him be holy still.

- Revelation 22:11

In death he was the same person he was as in life. If he didn't desire the attention of believers while on earth, he wouldn't desire the attention of believers after death. Having slipped outside of his dead body, paradise wasn't an option, hell had the only standing invitation. He quickly gravitated toward people of similar nature and character and entered through the portals of hell.

Just as he began to suffer he couldn't help but notice the many others who were likewise suffering. Any conversation he had with them didn't offer the least bit of hope. Those who had been there from previous centuries couldn't offer any encouragement. There was no end to the pain and no way of escape. Assessing his situation panic enveloped him. Looking this way, then that way; running here, running there; doing anything, going anywhere where the torment could possibly lessen, yet all to no avail.

All inquiries from those who shared his torment discovered the same hopelessness. No matter where in hell they explored it was all the same. All others they communicated with found the countless years to run together. Without the sun to take notice of, there were no such things as days, months, and years. Time just meshed into one conglomerate of existence.

I suppose the biggest surprise was that he was not only conscious, *but that he was conscious with faculties that corresponded to his physical body on earth.* Many people wrongly assume that being out of the physical body means they'll resemble, in appearance, puffs of smoke similar to the cartoon ghost Casper. This is incorrect. Let's examine the spirit body of this rich man.

The Rich Man's Spirit Body

And in hell he lift up his EYES, being in torments, and SEETH Abraham afar off...
- Luke 16:23

The first thing we notice about his body in hell is that he had *eyes*. With these eyes he was able to *see*. He was even able to see things that were a great distance away:

...and seeth Abraham AFAR OFF...

Evidently his eyes had excellent vision and perception. The next thing we notice is that he talked:

And he cried and SAID, Father Abraham...
- Luke 16:24

He didn't communicate telepathically. He didn't read the other's mind. He and Abraham *said* words to each other. Further, when he talked he talked with a loud voice:

And he CRIED and said...

Clearly, he was *yelling* to Abraham across a great gulf. He was talking very loudly because either there was a lot of noise in that area to overcome or because of the great distance Abraham was away. Probably it was a combination of both. Since he was able to talk, the others there were able to talk as well. With all those on his side of the gulf being in torment there was probably much weeping and wailing, with much noise to overcome. Then he said:

...Father Abraham, have mercy on me, and send Lazarus, that he may dip the tip of his FINGER in water, and cool my TONGUE;

- Luke 16:24

Now we notice a finger and a tongue. Obviously the finger wasn't aimlessly floating around in the air. It was attached to a hand which, in turn, was attached to an arm which, in turn, was attached to a torso. Likewise, his tongue wasn't floating in the air away from where he was. It, too, was attached to his body, or more specifically, his mouth. Further, with his tongue he was able to *taste*. The water would have brought cool refreshment to him.

Already we see that this man's body in hell was similar in appearance to his earthly body. In addition, he was able to *recognize* Lazarus with Abraham on the other side of the great gulf. Having seen Lazarus laid at his gate every day on earth he easily recognized him in the spirit world. To the person with an open mind it seems that our spirits look just like our physical bodies. *Yes, there is recognition on the other side of death.* Why? Because we look just like we do now. The only difference is that our spirit bodies are free from the imperfections of this fallen, physical world. If we don't have an arm here we will have it on the other side.

With this spirit body he was also able to *feel*:

...for I am TORMENTED in this flame.

His spirit body was able to *feel* torment while Lazarus' body was able to feel comfort. Evidently, what brings comfort to our bodies on earth brings comfort to our spirit body in the spirit world. What brings pain to our bodies on earth likewise brings pain to our spirit body in the spirit world.

We next notice that he had *memory*:

But Abraham said, Son, REMEMBER that thou in thy lifetime receivedst thy good things, and likewise Lazarus evil things: but now he is comforted, and thou art tormented.
- Luke 16:25

His mind was able to think back to his former life on earth. He could remember how he was able to enjoy luxury previous to being in hell. He could yearn for the old days when life seemed good to him. I would think, though, that those memories would be a curse to him, for they could never more be.

We also learn that the spirit body doesn't fly:

And beside all this, between us and you there is a great gulf fixed: so that they which would pass from hence to you cannot; neither can they pass to us, that would come from thence.

- Luke 16:26

If they could fly in the spirit world this great gulf would not have been a hindrance. They would have just levitated over the gulf through the air to where the area of comfort was. Just as gravity on earth keeps our bodies to the surface there is a similar force in hell that keeps spirits out of the air. They must be bound to moving about by walking with similar gravitational laws.

We also see great *concern* from the inhabitants of hell for their unsaved loved ones on earth. Their *emotions* are still intact in hell:

Then he said, I pray thee therefore, father (Abraham), that thou wouldest send him (Lazarus) to my father's house: For I have five brethren; that he may testify unto them, lest they also come into this place of torment.

- Luke 16:27-28

Hell was so distasteful, so painful, and so fearful to this rich man that he couldn't bear the thought of his five brothers ending up where he was. Often we hear the unsaved mockingly say that they want to go to hell to be with their friends, but those people already in hell don't want their friends to join them. Their torment is too great for there to be any camaraderie. Hell is not a place where any happiness is possible. To be rejoined with friends and loved ones in hell doesn't bring any pleasing thoughts to their minds. The nature of their existence is so difficult to deal with moment by moment that having to visit with their so-called friends brings further anguish to their thinking. All they can think about is getting through each horrendous moment after the other.

It is to be regretted now that it's too late for anything to be done for this rich man, but oddly enough, he now has an evangelistic heart. He obviously had genuine concern for his five brothers. He truly didn't want them to end up where he was. But, alas, nothing could be done for them except what had been likewise available to him — God's Word.

Abraham said unto him, they have Moses and the prophets (God's Word); let them hear them. And he said, Nay, father Abraham: but if one went unto them from the dead, they will repent. And he said unto him, If they hear not Moses and the prophets (God's Word), neither will they be persuaded, though one rose from the dead.
- Luke 16:29-31

The deluded thinking of so many is that if a known personality who was dead came back to life, the unsaved would immediately repent and believe. According to Abraham, though, even if someone arose from the dead, the unsaved would not be persuaded. This is difficult for some to grasp, but true nonetheless.

For example, if George Washington came back to life and proclaimed in front of the media he was back from the dead, do we really think that people would accept this? Of course not. They would think he was either a great impersonator out to dupe the masses or a psychotic nut who needed to be in a mental hospital. Most people would be offended that he would be expecting them to actually believe he was who he claimed to be. Others would think it was a charade and play along for good sport. A few of the lunatic fringe might believe him, but their belief in him would probably hurt his credibility all the more.

If someone from our modern era returned from the dead the greater portion of the world would think he had never been dead to begin with, perhaps a conspiracy to befuddle the masses. They would be upset with him for having pretended to be dead while they had mourned and grieved his "mock" funeral — *"How dare he trifle with our emotions by playing such a cruel trick?"* If he talked about heaven and hell or had a message from God to them, they would think he had staged his "death" for his supposed reappearance. He would be regarded as a religious quack.

Without any doubt, the only thing with the capability to convince people of their need for spiritual salvation is the Word of God. God's Word has the power built into it to change the hearts of men. If people won't believe God's Word nothing can be done for them and, like this rich man, face a hideous future on the other side of the grave.

For I am not ashamed of the gospel of Christ: for *it is the power of God unto salvation* **to every one that**

believeth...

Something else to consider here is that perhaps he didn't want to be rejoined with his five brothers because they might blame him for their spiritual condition. It's certainly within the realm of possibility that his selfish lifestyle had set the tone the others ended up following. Younger brothers and sisters are heavily influenced, right or wrong, by the lifestyle of the elder siblings. Perhaps his neglect of spiritual matters wrongly influenced his brothers to ignore God and the teachings of the religious leaders in their community. If his self-centered life caused his brothers to follow in his footsteps he may not want to see them to hear their eternal accusations. Abrasive and hostile recriminations awaited him with their reunion.

For example, surely those who followed Hitler in his suicidal death pact will impugn him in hell. He will not only suffer the torment of hell, whatever that may encompass, but in the midst of that he will also face the raw hatred of those who went to hell solely because of his influence. Further, those who were killed because of his command on earth, if they were unsaved and went to hell, will likewise incriminate him as well. Hitler's hell will be far worse than many others (degrees of punishment will be discussed in chapter 11).

There are no happy reunions in hell. Former friends will blame each other for the peer pressure that was exerted on them that kept them from church. The negative impact of famous personalities that kept many from making decisions for Christ will come back to haunt their existence in hell.

There will be no compassion and no understanding, only hostility, malice, and disgust.

...he that believeth not shall be damned.
- Mark 16:16

The truest definition of hell is damnation. Damnation and hell are synonymous. To be damned is to be in hell, to be in hell is to be damned. For people to think that hell will be a continuation of a party they started on earth is foreign to the thinking of hell's inhabitants. This rich man couldn't think of anything other than the smallest drop of water to minutely relieve his intolerable condition.

CHAPTER
3

The Strange Request Of
The Rich Man

And he cried and said, Father Abraham, have mercy on me, and send Lazarus, that he may dip the tip of his finger in water, and cool my tongue; for I am tormented in this flame.

- Luke 16:24

At first glance it doesn't seem strange asking for water to cool a tongue if the one asking is suffering in a flame. Yet after further thought, considering the awful torment this man is experiencing, it seems ridiculously minuscule to *only* ask for Lazarus to dip the tip of his finger in water to cool his tongue. Why such a small request? Wouldn't it make more sense to ask for something on a larger scale? Why not a *cup* of water? Or for 5 minutes out of the torment? Or 10 minutes? Or a half hour? Why not ask if there was any way possible to get out of the torment permanently? That he might somehow be able to enter paradise?

Based on his small request it seems that he didn't entertain any hope of ever getting out of hell. It almost appears that he considers himself unfit for paradise. As if he rightly recognized his spiritual condition as being his own fault. As if he realized his nature wouldn't allow him association anywhere outside of hell. Almost as if he was made for hell, or more accurately, as if hell was made for him and, in paradise, he would be in even worse torment.

I mean, why didn't he ask to enter paradise? Unless, that is, he already understood the nature of his suffering as being his *condition* rather than his *location*. Is it not possible that his torment had no relation to *where* he was but, instead, to *what* he was? If so, this gives us further insight as to why Jesus told us that we must be born again. There must be something hideously wrong with the spiritual nature of the unsaved.

The words "born again," which are even being used today in some parts of the secular world, are more than a catch phrase they've latched on to. It is talking about an actual *second* birth, the birth of the human spirit. To live physically we must have a physical birth. To live spiritually we must have a *spiritual* birth. The person who does not experience the spiritual birth is not alive, but dead — spiritually dead, that is. This is why just trying to be a good person is not enough to take a person to heaven. Their inside spiritual nature has to change. They must be *born* a child of God.

It's important to realize that we don't *gradually* become children of God. In other words, we don't try to get better and better until we finally attain the status of being

God's children. Human reasoning thinks that if we modify our behavior we'll eventually change our inside. The truth is, though, we've only formed good habits. As important as good habits are, they do nothing for the *spirit* of man. Ultimate change doesn't come from the outside in, but from the inside out.

For example, many think that if they attend church on a regular basis they become Christians. However, sitting in a church doesn't make one a Christian anymore than sitting in a barn would make one a cow. To become a cow one has to be born a cow, and to become a Christian one has to be born a Christian. This doesn't mean being born into a family whose parents are Christians, but rather experiencing a spiritual birth by receiving Jesus Christ as the Lord of your life.

When a person receives Jesus Christ as his Lord and Savior, something marvelous happens on the *inside* of him. After prayer he may look like the same person, but he is actually a *brand new* person:

Therefore if any man be in Christ, he is a NEW creation: old things are passed away; behold, ALL THINGS ARE BECOME NEW.

- 2 Corinthians 5:17

In other words, the mind and body are still the same, but the *spirit* of man was instantly *born* a child of Almighty God. His mannerisms are still the same, his accent is still the same, his demeanor is still the same, his memories are still the same, but *spiritually* he is truly a brand new baby. Because he is instantly different on the *inside*, he will gradually change on the *outside*. He's not trying to be good on the outside to become a different person on the inside, he's progressively becoming good on the outside because he's already a different person on the inside.

This inside change is being born *again*. This *new* birth, this spiritual birth, is every bit as supernatural as the physical birth is natural. His nature on the inside of him is now just like his spiritual Father. He may not look it on this side of the grave, but on the other side his spiritual nature is easily apparent. Over there he looks every bit the child of God that he is.

This disclosure brings us back to this rich man in hell. He never experienced such a change in his spirit. As a result, his spirit was out of harmony with the spirits in paradise. He doesn't look like a child of God over there simply because he's not. His nature is a fallen nature. Because of what took place in the garden of Eden at the fall of Adam and Eve, without Christ, our natures are cursed. They are sick and diseased, so to speak. Actually, the reason we must be born again is because our spirits are dead.

People don't go to hell because God is out to get them. People go to hell because their spiritual nature is dead. They're not in the family. To go to heaven one must be a child of God. Otherwise, they're still in the devil's family:

Ye are of your father the devil, and the lusts of your father ye will do...

- John 8:44

People go to hell, not because God doesn't love them, but because they don't have the nature of God in them. They haven't had life imparted to their spirit. This is why God sent Jesus to pay the penalty for mankind's sin. God loved the world so much that He sent His only begotten Son, so that whosoever would believe on Jesus should not perish, but have everlasting life (John 3:16). To not receive Jesus is to remain in the condition of spiritual death. As such, they are unfit for heaven.

Further, their nature is diseased (technically, it is dead, but because most look at death as meaning the cessation of existence, I'm using the term diseased to make a point). Generally speaking, disease, without medication, has pain associated with it. It's the physical condition that results in the physical suffering. *Likewise, it is the spiritual condition that results in the spiritual suffering.* Just as hospitals on earth have certain wards to quarantine the diseased from the healthy, so does God have a ward called hell to quarantine the spiritually diseased from the spiritually healthy. The nature of their suffering is associated with the pains of fire. We get a glimpse of this in the following scripture about Satan's fall.

...therefore will I bring forth a fire FROM THE MIDST OF THEE, it shall devour thee...
- Ezekiel 28:18

The fire that Satan was going to suffer would come from the *inside* of him. This is a scary thought. There is nowhere to run, nowhere to hide, and nowhere to escape to. The fire is always present because it is *inside*. It burns and burns and burns and burns. Isaiah adds to this concerning

41

unregenerate man by saying:

And they shall go forth, and look upon the carcases of the men that have transgressed against me: for their worm shall not die, neither shall THEIR FIRE be quenched;

- Isaiah 66:24

This is not to say that there are not other kinds of fire in hell (see chapters 9 and 10 about the fire of hell). This is mentioned only to deepen the dread of that which is already revealed to be there. For example, many years ago I suffered the ordeal of passing a kidney stone. Kidney stones are grainy particles that form in the kidney. Occasionally, they can be very large. At some point they enter the ureter to leave the kidney en route to the bladder. If the stone is too large to pass easily, the severe, constant pain continues as the muscles in the walls of the tiny ureter try to squeeze the stone along into the bladder. Further, many of the stones have jagged edges. When the stone is introduced to the ureter is when the *horrid* pain begins.

I don't want to over-exaggerate this mind boggling pain that never eases, but many women compare the passing of a kidney stone to birthing a baby. When the baby is ready to leave the womb en route to the outside world, the mother's passageway is much too small to allow easy passage. As a result, the pain can be almost overbearing at times to handle.

With both of these conditions there is a tearing on the inside of the body. A ripping, if you will. Some compare it to a *burning* as the flesh tears. This pain can be sharp at times, dull at times, but it never eases until something passes. To be in labor for 24 to 48 hours with its resultant pain is difficult for some to deal with. This is one reason why in years gone by many women died in childbirth. It was just too much pain for the physical body to endure.

Imagine, though, that if the stone would *never* pass, or if the baby would *never* be delivered, *what suffering would be endured!* Then amplify that pain 1,000 fold and we still haven't come close to understanding the burning those in hell are suffering. It's just too bizarre to adequately explain and comprehend. It never stops. It always burns. And there is no remedy.

My point here is to help people understand that God isn't damning people. *Their damnation is a result of their spiritually dead nature.* God didn't make hell to damn the unsaved. God made hell to house those already damned. Actually, it's the mercy of God displayed in that He made this special ward for the unsaved. Should the unsaved not be in hell, their suffering would be ineffable. Let me explain.

The spirits of the unsaved are out of tune with the intonation of heaven. What is harmony to those in heaven is *out of tune* to those in hell. Because heaven is pure joy and because hell is pure evil, should an inhabitant of hell enter into heaven, the pureness of heaven's melody to the unsaved would be like hearing fingernails scratching on a chalkboard at 140 decibels on an unending basis. The continual "screeching" would be abhorrent to their spiritual nature. The unsaved would quickly reach back to areas in tune with their discordant nature.

Hell

Jesus often compared the saved and unsaved with light and darkness. To prison inmates locked away in the "hole" of a prison, those certain prisoners will spend days and sometimes weeks locked in a cell without any light. Alone and in perpetual darkness, they quickly lose touch with the outside world. After days of confinement in such cells, without any comprehension of time, the prison guards suddenly spring open the cell door. The outside light immediately rushes in, and because the pupils can't dilate fast enough to handle the instant surge of light, the eyes are temporarily blinded. The inmate immediately cowers from the light and reaches to the corners of the cell where he might escape this bright intruder.

Similarly, the spiritual nature of the unsaved is darkness, and the spiritual nature of the saved is light. In the spirit world the two can't intermingle. Should the unsaved enter heaven, the light would overwhelm and overpower them. Though on earth we can gradually adjust to light, in the spirit world the unsaved can't ever adjust to the light *because their nature is total darkness.* The continual light would be torturous to their spiritual nature. The unsaved would immediately gravitate back to areas of darkness.

In this we can see demonstrated the goodness and mercy of God. The very nature of the unsaved is difficult to conceive. Their torment in that flame never stops burning and the resultant pain must be harrowing. However, if they would enter heaven their spiritual suffering would enter into realms beyond intolerable. Therefore, God created hell to quarantine the living dead from all universal light. In hell the unrighteous can mingle with kindred spirits.

Evidently, this rich man already understood this. He didn't ask to be released from hell because he knew he was unable to be anywhere other than hell. Any place else was a spiritual impossibility. His nature wouldn't allow him access outside the boundaries of hell. The borders were "fixed" and unable to be crossed. Further, the water that Lazarus would have brought to him, had it been permitted, wouldn't have alleviated his tongue anyway. Anything from regions of light would only have caused anguish to those in regions of darkness.

The inhabitants of hell don't blame God for their suffering. They understand that their agonizing suffering is the result of their nature. Yes, God sends the unsaved to hell, but not for the reasons the world attributes to Him. They look at God as being an ogre who wants to spiritually destroy people. Nothing could be further from the truth. God sends the unsaved to hell because, in their condition of spiritual death, anywhere else would be impossible. As bad as their suffering is in hell, in heaven it would be far worse. The inhabitants of hell recognize the justice of God, the goodness of God, and the mercy of God.

This is why it's so utterly foolish to say, *"I don't want to be in heaven with a God who sends people to hell. I would rather go to hell to defy Him."* They are ignorantly blaming God for the misery of hell's inhabitants. The truth is, the misery of hell's inhabitants is not because of God, but because of their spiritually diseased nature. If it wasn't for the mercy of God there wouldn't be a hell. The unsaved's suffering would be on a scale beyond measuring. Surprising to most, hell is Love's response to the spiritual *condition* of the unredeemed.

SECTION 2

HELL

WHERE? WHAT? WHY? WHO?

CHAPTER
4

Where Is Hell?

...what is it but that he also descended first into the
lower parts of the earth...

- Ephesians 4:9

Hell is located in the lower parts of the earth. Yet if we had the ability to drill from the earth's crust down to the earth's core we would certainly find extreme heat, but we wouldn't find hell. The reason is because hell is not a *physical* place. When unsaved people die their physical bodies are buried in the earth and their *spirits* go into hell. Thus, hell is a *spiritual* place. Yet this spiritual abode has its location in the lower parts of this physical earth.

Don't be confused by the term a *spiritual* place. Many people think that unless a place is a *physical* place, anything else must not be real. The truth is, anything spiritual is just as real as anything physical, actually more so. This physical world was patterned after that which is in the spiritual world.

People have erroneous concepts about the world of the spirit. Some think that people over there float on clouds and play harps. Nothing could be further from the truth. In the world of the spirit there are houses (John 14:2), streets (Rev. 21:21), gates (Rev. 21:12,21), and precious stones and minerals (Rev. 21:19-20). The people living there wear clothes (Rev. 1:13, 7:9,13), eat fruit from trees (Rev.22:2), have hair (Rev. 1:14), have bodies with eyes, mouths, arms, hands, legs, and feet (Luke 16: 23-25, Rev. 1:13-16), and sit in chairs (Rev. 4:4) There are animals (Rev. 19:11), water to drink from fountains (Rev.2:6), and vehicles of transportation (2 Kings 2:11).

The world of the spirit is similar to this physical world, the difference being that it is in another dimension, so to speak. The point is, with all the advancements and ultra sensitive equipment science has devised, hell will never be discovered by *natural* means. Similarly, heaven will never be discovered by telescopes, radio waves, etc. Heaven, too, is a *spiritual* place. Spiritual things can't be seen or touched by physical things. For a person to refuse to believe in heaven or hell simply because science hasn't "proven" their existence is the worst mistake one could make.

Hell is a very real place. It is not a state of mind. It is not an unending psychological nightmare. Nor is it emotional trauma. It is an actual place, just as real as Los Angeles, London, and Tokyo. It has a population of inhabitants who at one time lived on the earth or in heaven. Every hour its population grows as the unsaved people on earth die. During times of war or plague, its population increases rapidly and hell expands (Isaiah 5:14). Many scriptures refer to hell as being down:

go *down* quick into hell	**Psalm 86:13**
depart from hell *beneath*	**Proverb 15:24**
hell from *beneath*	**Isaiah 14:9**
brought *down* to hell	**Isaiah 14:14, 57:9, Matthew 11:23**
cast *down* to hell	**Ezekiel 31:16-17, Luke 10:15, 2 Peter 2:4**
gone *down* to hell	**Ezekiel 32:27**

When an unsaved person dies, they slip out of their physical body and immediately gravitate downward. They find themselves plummeting away from the lights of the earth down into outer darkness. The further they go the darker it gets. When they arrive at the entrance of hell they find there to be gates:

...the gates of hell shall not prevail against it...
- Matthew 16:18

Once they pass through hell's gates they will be confined until their final judgment, the lake of fire. Their eternal destiny will be fixed, never to be changed. No hope, no parole, and no escape. Jesus gave us further information as to hell's location:

For as Jonah was three days and three nights in the whale's belly; so shall the Son of man be three days

and three nights in the HEART OF THE EARTH.
- Matthew 12:40

Hell, then, is located in close proximity to the center of the earth. Since scientific equipment is incapable of "finding" hell to be there, it could be said that hell is simply in another dimension, a dimension other than this physical world. To be scripturally correct, though, hell is in the world of the spirit.

It's important to realize that man is a *spiritual* being encased in a *physical* body. As such, we touch two worlds — the spirit world and this earthly, natural world. It has been said that our physical bodies are earth-suits, so to speak. As long as we remain in our earth-suits we can live on the earth. However, when we step out of our earth-suits we can no longer live in this natural world, we transfer to the spirit world.

Thus, when people die and, to use our analogy, step out of their earth-suits, they leave this part of the earth where the sun shines, step over into another dimension called the spirit world, and descend into the lower parts of the earth called hell. Passing through hell's gates, they will never see the earth again.

CHAPTER 5

What Is Hell?

For Christ also hath once suffered for sins ... being put to death in the flesh, but quickened by the Spirit: By which also he went and preached unto the spirits in PRISON;

- 1 Peter 3:18-19

Hell is a spiritual prison, plain and simple. It is a jail to confine outlaw and reprobate spirits. Without it there would be universal anarchy and rebellion. Hell is ugly, because perpetual wickedness and evil when allowed to roam free is uglier.

One difficulty we have living in this natural world is that we can't see evil for what it truly is. We get glimpses of it in the lives of the Hitlers and the Stalins of the world, and the rapists, perverts, deviants, and murderers, but even at that, it is veiled. The flesh mutes the sordid wickedness of the heart. When these individuals just mentioned stepped outside of their physical bodies, there was nothing to disguise their every intent. They became personified evil.

As disgusting as evil is in this world, it is amplified a thousandfold in the world of the spirit. At present we can't comprehend what is in the nature of unregenerate mankind. This is why Jesus said that we must be born again (John 3:5-7). Without Jesus we have a fallen nature and, thus, our natures have to change. As long as we're in the flesh we can't see the truest manifestation of that evil. It's not until a person dies and is released of their physical body that their nature is free to express itself to its fullest.

If one would go into the most dangerous, darkest, maximum security prison here on earth and observe the deranged, psychotic, criminal element behind bars, we still couldn't fully grasp the evil manifested in the world of the spirit. Satan is truly a lunatic. What we find in our worst earthly penitentiary is only a shadow of the rampant evil expressed amongst the unsaved in the spirit world. Those who have died without being born again become free to manifest that which was in their heart. They become evil incarnate.

With multiplied millions of evil, unregenerate human spirits presently in the spirit world they cannot be allowed to roam free. Thus, in the mind of God, a prison was conceived — hell. Evil had to be restrained. Wickedness had to be bound. If people choose evil over good God allows them their choice, but not *where* they can practice it. Evil spirits must be separated from holy, righteous spirits.

In the not too distant future Satan and his demons will be cast into the lake of fire separated from all universal good. The universe will one day be purged of all evil. However, for man, his probation is his life on earth. When his life draws to a close, his eternal judgment is set. Hell is the place designated by God for the unsaved to exist separate from the saved until the day that death and hell are cast into the lake of fire (Revelation 20:14). Righteous spirits cannot cross over to be with the unrighteous, and the unrighteous cannot cross over to be with the righteous. Hell is an area that is secluded for reprobate spirits.

No Escape From Hell

Escape is an impossibility. For example, suppose a prison was built in the middle of the Atlantic Ocean 10,000 feet below sea level. If an inmate could somehow get on the outside of the walls of that prison it would actually be worse for him than being on the inside of that prison. The enormous pressure of the water 10,000 feet below sea level would cause excruciating suffering and certain death. Swimming the two miles to the surface would be an impossibility.

Even if someone could obtain a pressurized diving suit, imagine further that there would not be a surface to swim to. No matter what direction the escapee would swim there would be nothing but water. Sooner or later the oxygen would run out, the suit would collapse under the intense pressure and his horrific death would ensue. Of course, many inmates would prefer death, no matter how agonizing, over the hideous, unending life in prison.

One problem with this analogy is that death could be an alternative to prison life. In hell there isn't such a thing as death, that is, in the sense of ending it all. In hell the option of ending it all can never take place, the confinement is fixed, and escape is impossible. Hell is fast, furious, and unrelenting. Once in, there is no way out.

Just as gravity keeps us on the earth, there is, for a lack of a better explanation, a "spiritual gravity" that keeps the unsaved in hell. There is an unseen force that keeps the sinner from ever leaving hell. On earth we can build vehicles to supercede the law of gravity by exercising the law of lift. However, in hell there are no means to build similar vehicles that would allow escape from hell. In hell there are no metals to dig for, no ores to be mined, and no iron in which to make tools. Without materials to build vehicles and without tools in which to craft such vehicles, there is not a vehicle that could be made to supercede this so-called spiritual gravity to get out of hell. Even if God would have allowed such materials to be found in hell (which there are not), again, there is nowhere to escape to. Hell is in a dimension from which there is no escape.

Hell is utterly hopeless. For those in hell to hope for a pardon causes even further anguish, for they know there is no pardon. On earth a person in pain can at least look forward to a brief respite with a dose of codeine, morphine, or aspirin. However brief the relief, at least it is some kind of relief. Unfortunately, in hell there is no relief of any kind, no matter how brief from the constant torment. It never stops and never eases.

The word "forever" is difficult to grasp with the finite mind. We're used to beginnings and endings. Dealing with a subject in which there is no end causes the mind to tilt. The justice of God is then brought into question, *"How could a loving God allow hell and the eventual lake of fire?"* However, this question could easily be turned around. For the people who love God and live for God, how could a loving God allow evil beings to forever be free to harass and intimidate holy and righteous beings? Wouldn't that be unfair to the righteous? Of course it would.

Thus, in the mind of God, hell was made to quarantine the unrighteous from the righteous until the final judgment. In this way, the righteous are free to worship the God they adore and forever fellowship with each other, and the unrighteous are able to exist away from the God they rejected and live their debased wickedness amongst themselves. Hell is just as much their condition as it is their prison.

CHAPTER
6

Why Is There A Hell?

God is a God of justice. It is unfair to preach about the love of God without also preaching about the justice of God. Yes, God loves everyone, but as we learn from what is written about the people of Noah's day, God will not always strive with man (Genesis 6:3). If man continues to reject God and spurn His love, eventually God's mercy will come to an end as far as they are concerned, and judgment will ensue. However, God doesn't get any pleasure in the death of the wicked:

For I (God) have no pleasure in the death of him (the sinner) that dieth, saith the Lord God: wherefore turn yourselves, and live ye.
- Ezekiel 18:32

It is a sad day when an unsaved person dies. They chose to live a life devoid of any thought with eternal ramifications. They lived only for this life, not for the life which is to come. God had such great expectations for them and wanted to be a father to them, but, for whatever reason, they didn't want to be a part of God's family. Self-will was more important to them than God's will.

It's important to realize that God will honor the choice of each and every person. If certain people do not want to have anything to do with God, God will not force them to love Him. God does not make people do what they don't want to do. Should people decide to reject God and His way of life, God allows them to follow their own course. God doesn't make people go to heaven. However, if they refuse God, they are also refusing all of His creation, which is heaven, earth, and the created universe. Therefore, a place had to be created specially for those who would prefer life without God. This place is called hell.

When God created man He didn't want robots or pets. He wanted a creation worthy of fellowshipping with his Creator. God wanted someone just like Himself — someone who could think on his own, be creative, spontaneous, witty, and highly intelligent. When God created Adam and Eve He had such people. All generations born from this union would be His family on earth. Earth was to be man's version of God's heaven — a carbon copy, if you will. Heaven was to be God's home and earth was to be man's home (Psalm 115:16).

The possibilities for mankind were limitless. The universe was man's backyard. What he could conceive he could do. Mankind was made for productivity, accomplishment, and fellowship. Life was to be fulfilling, exciting, and purposeful. Men were to be husbands and fathers. Women were to be wives and mothers. Together, as a loving family, they were to discover their God-given dream and pursue it.

Unfortunately, in creating beings like this, the creation

could use this wonderful gift called life for purposes other than what God intended, even evil purposes. People have asked, *"Why would God create beings that could do wrong?"* The answer is simple enough — If God created beings who would only do what they were programmed to do, they wouldn't be like Himself, they would be robots. They might have flesh and blood, but they'd be just as hollow sounding as a metallic robot.

God wanted to create a people where he wouldn't know what they would say or do, beings who could surprise Him, make Him laugh. He wanted people where He could plant a dream on the inside of them and let them choose how to go about accomplishing it. He wanted people who could think, plan, and pursue. But by creating beings with such unlimited potential, paradoxically, they would also have the ability to reject the very One who afforded them life. In God's view this was a risk worth taking.

Of course, God provided mankind with everything that they could ever hope, dream, or desire. Mankind's every whim was prepared for before they had even been created. With the exception of just one tree, the *whole* world had been given to them. Think about this — the entire earth had been given to man. There wasn't a need for man to yield to a tempter, for everything already belonged to him. His present and future could be molded to become any kind of life *he* wanted it to be.

However, Adam and Eve ignored the whole of the creation and, ridiculously, chose to disobey God and pursue the *one* tree that was off limits. In so doing they doomed the whole race. Man's unlimited potential died on that particular day. Life, if such a word could now be used, was relegated to death, despair, and hopelessness. The earth now had a new lord and master — Satan.

Man was created as a spirit being, with a soul (mind, will, and emotions), encased in a physical body. God made man to live eternally. When a man or woman dies, the truth is, it is only their *physical* body that has died. The spirit and soul live on in another location — heaven or hell. Because man has been created to live forever, should he reject the God who created him, he has to exist somewhere. Heaven is an impossibility. Earth, too, is an impossibility. Therefore, a third place had to be created.

Unrighteous beings cannot exist with righteous beings. It is only in this present age that the unrighteous and righteous exist side by side. In the age to come, this will come to an end. Hell was created by God to separate the unrighteous from the righteous. The righteous will be free to live the life they desire and the unrighteous will be separated to be with those whose discordant natures are similar to their own.

Persecution and intimidation by the unrighteous on the righteous exists only in this world. In the next world God sees to it that this comes to an end by jailing the unrighteous away from the righteous. If the unrighteous don't want to have anything to do with a godly lifestyle, God answers their request by keeping them away from all that represents God.

Hell is necessary. On earth prisons keep the unsavory and criminal element away from the normal society. It wouldn't be fair to the rest of the population to allow murderers, rapists, perverts, and thieves free to practice their degraded lifestyle that would harm the innocent, honest, and hard working people. Murderers cannot be free to murder. Rapists cannot be free to rape. Perverts cannot be free to sodomize. Thieves cannot be free to steal.

Similarly, spirit beings cannot be free to practice their unrestrained evil in the spirit world. It wouldn't be fair to allow the children of the devil (John 8:44) to mingle with the children of God. The unsaved have chosen an eternal condition that the saved abhor. The saved don't want to be around the mitigated evil that the unsaved practice and, the truth is, the unsaved don't want to be around a godly life that is, to them, repulsive. Thus, in the mind of God, hell was logical, practical, and necessary.

CHAPTER 7

Who Was The Lake Of Fire Created For?

Then shall he say also unto them on the left hand, Depart from me, ye cursed, into everlasting fire, PREPARED FOR THE DEVIL AND HIS ANGELS:
- Matthew 25:41

Presently, as previously brought out, the unredeemed dead are existing in *hades*. Eventually, though, they will join Satan and his angels in the lake of fire, the final judgment. According to Jesus, the lake of fire was not made for man, but was made for the devil, fallen angels, and demons. Sometime prior to the creation of man another group of beings called angels had been created. Among this innumerable host (Hebrews 12:22), certain angels had been designated by God to lead. The known angelic leaders are Michael, Gabriel, and Lucifer. Certainly there are more than these, but we learn from this that there is rank and order among the angels.

However, Lucifer somehow became dissatisfied with

his role and led a revolt to usurp the throne of God. His vie for the throne was unsuccessful, and he and his cohorts were kicked out of heaven to the earth. There is evidently a set time yet in the future in which the devil and demons will be cast into the lake of fire. Notice:

And, behold, they cried out, saying, What have we to do with thee, Jesus, thou Son of God? Art thou come hither to torment us BEFORE THE TIME?
- Matthew 8:29

Satan, fallen angels, and demons are still hopelessly fighting to overthrow the kingdom of God. God, who knows the beginning from the end, the One who can see the future, has already told us that, at the end of this age of grace, Satan and demons will be removed from the earth and cast into the lake of fire. The lake of fire was specifically created for them. It is a shame that, after this life, *people* would exist in a place that was never intended for them to be. Yet, every day, people die, leave the earth, enter into hell, and eventually will join Satan in the lake of fire.

Because the lake of fire was created for Satan and his angels, we surmise that it was made sometime after Satan's revolt yet before the creation of man. Man was originally intended to live eternally on the earth in close fellowship with his heavenly Father. But when man turned his God-given authority over to Satan in his fall, Satan became the god of this world:

In whom the GOD OF THIS WORLD hath blinded the minds of them which believe not, lest the light

of the glorious gospel of Christ, who is the image of God, should shine unto them.
- 2 Corinthians 4:4

In fact, according to Jesus, unregenerate mankind is a part of Satan's family:

YE are of your father the devil, and the lusts of your father ye will do...
- John 8:44

Evidently, when man dies, if Jesus is his lord, he'll spend his eternity with his lord and enjoy the corresponding reward. If man rejects the lordship of Jesus, then Satan is his lord, and when he dies he'll spend his eternity with his lord and experience the corresponding judgment.

Since the lake of fire was built to confine Satan and those angels who pledged allegiance to him and his rebellion, when man, in his fall in the garden of Eden, bowed his knee to Satan his spiritual allegiance was eternally linked to Satan. Therefore, the lake of fire now encompasses *all* who reject the plan of God — Satan, fallen angels, *and unregenerate man.* Unsaved mankind will share its future with all those beings who chose rebellion, anarchy, and self-will, because man, without Jesus, is just like them.

People ask, *"How come the lake of fire is eternal when life on earth is only 70 or so years long, many times much less than that? It seems unjust for a person to be judged eternally for a life that is comparatively so short."*

This answer is easy. Think about a murderer who is serving a life sentence in a prison. The actual murder that he committed took 5 minutes or less. Yet his 99 year life sentence isn't based on the short length of time it took to commit the murder, the sentence was based on the gravity of the crime. *Likewise, the eternity of the lake of fire isn't based on how long a life of sin was lived on earth, it is based on the gravity of the sin condition.*

It's important to realize that the eventual lake of fire isn't based on the different forms that sin may take on. People sin in many different ways. The issue is not the *kinds* of sin, but the sin itself. The world has failed to realize the hideousness of sin. Sin is repulsive to God. It is a cancer. How sin is manifested is as different as there are people. So it's not *how* sin is manifested that is disgusting to God, it's that there is sin.

Our life on earth is simply a probation. 70 or 80 years is more than sufficient to determine the course a person will choose. Generally, 15 to 25 years is sufficient for most. People's conscious awareness may not be manifest, but down in their spirit, in their innermost being, most decide what God means to them before they even think about the occupation they'll engage in the rest of their earthly days. Very early in life people decide how they'll live spiritually. This probationary decision is an eternal decision.

SECTION 3

SCRIPTURAL FACTS ABOUT HELL, THE LAKE OF FIRE, AND ETERNITY

CHAPTER 8

Sheol, Hades, and Gehenna
(The Difference Between Hades and the Lake of Fire)

There are several words translated hell in the Bible. The Old Testament word translated hell is *sheol*. Several examples are as follows:

For a fire is kindled in mine anger, and shall burn unto the lowest hell (sheol)...

- Deuteronomy 32:22

Hell (sheol) is naked before him...

- Job 26:6

The wicked shall be turned into hell (sheol), and all the nations that forget God.

- Psalm 9:17

And your covenant with death shall be disan-

nulled, and your agreement with hell (sheol) shall not stand; when the overflowing scourge shall pass through, then ye shall be trodden down by it.

- Isaiah 28:18

Yet thou shalt be brought down to hell (sheol), to the sides of the pit.

- Isaiah 14:15

The New Testament word translated hell is *hades.* Several examples are as follows:

And in hell (hades) he lift up his eyes, being in torments...

- Luke 16:23

...and the gates of hell (hades) shall not prevail against it.

- Matthew 16:18

I am he that liveth, and was dead; and, behold, I am alive forevermore, Amen; and have the keys of hell (hades) and death.

- Revelation 1:18

And thou, Capernaum, which art exalted unto heaven, shalt be brought down to hell (hades).

- Matthew 11:23

And I looked and beheld a pale horse: and his name that sat on him was death, and hell (hades) followed

with him.

- Revelation 6:8

The Old Testament word *sheol* is the equivalent and counterpart to the New Testament word *hades*. *Hades* and *sheol* are one and the same. For example, the Spanish word for hell is *infierno*, and the French word for hell is *enfer*. We don't think that *infierno* and *enfer* are two different places. They are words in two different languages used to describe one and the same place.

Likewise, since the Old Testament was translated from the Hebrew language and the New Testament was translated from the Greek language, we understand that *sheol* and *hades* are not two different places. They are words in two different languages used to describe one and the same place.

The scriptures that best exemplify this truth are Psalm 16:10 and Acts 2:27. In Acts 2:27, the apostle Peter was quoting Psalm 16:10 concerning the resurrection of Jesus. Notice:

Because thou wilt not leave my soul in hell (hades), neither wilt thou suffer thine Holy One to see corruption.
- Acts 2:27

For thou wilt not leave my soul in hell (sheol); neither wilt thou suffer thine Holy One to see corruption.
- Psalm 16:10

Beyond any doubt, then, we see that *sheol* and *hades* are one and the same place. Another Greek word translated hell in the New Testament is *Gehenna*. Several examples are as follows:

And if thy hand offend thee, cut it off: it is better for thee to enter into life maimed, than having two hands to go into hell (Gehenna), into the fire that never shall be quenched...

- Mark 9:43

And fear not them which kill the body, but are not able to kill the soul; but rather fear him which is able to destroy both soul and body in hell (Gehenna).

- Matthew 10:28

Ye serpents, ye generation of vipers, how can ye escape the damnation of hell (Gehenna)?

- Matthew 23:33

...but whosoever shall say, Thou fool, shall be in danger of hell (Gehenna) fire.

- Matthew 5:22

...and not that thy whole body should be cast into hell (Gehenna).

- Matthew 5:29

Gehenna is not to be confused as being the same place as *hades*. *Hades* and *Gehenna* are two separate places. How do we know? Because the unsaved don't have their bodies while in *hades*. Only their spirit and soul is being confined in *hades*. Their bodies, which have been turned back to the dust of the earth for the time being, will be resurrected at the end of this age and then, according to Jesus, both soul *and body* will be cast into *Gehenna*. Notice:

> **And fear not them which kill the body, but are not able to kill the soul; but rather fear him which is able to destroy both soul AND BODY in Gehenna.**
> **- Matthew 10:28**

Gehenna, then, has nothing to do with the present incarceration of the wicked dead in *hades*, but rather to their future judgment. In a sense, we could say that *hades* is the county or state jail and *Gehenna* is the federal penitentiary. On earth the county jail houses the accused until the trial which, if found guilty, is sentenced by the judge to the penitentiary. Likewise, *hades* is where the unsaved are confined until the final judgment, at which point they will be cast into the lake of fire.

At the final judgment in front of the supreme Judge the unsaved will be rejoined with their bodies as we saw from Matthew 10:28. The prophet Daniel said it this way:

> **And many of them THAT SLEEP IN THE DUST OF THE EARTH** (their dead bodies) **SHALL AWAKE** (come back to life)**, some to everlasting life, AND SOME TO SHAME AND EVERLASTING CONTEMPT.**
> **- Daniel 12:2**

We see that *hades* is going to one day give up its inhabitants to stand before the great white throne of God:

> **...and death and hell delivered up the dead which**

were in them: and they judged every man according to their works.

- Revelation 20:13

Once they are then judged by God they will be cast into the lake of fire:

And death and hell were cast into the lake of fire. This is the second death. And whosoever was not found written in the book of life was cast into the lake of fire.
- Revelation 20:14

This lake of fire is the place Jesus called *Gehenna*. *Gehenna* was a term the Jews were well acquainted with in Jesus' day. They were already using it to describe the place for the final retribution of the wicked. It was a valley outside Jerusalem called Hinnom where, at one time, human sacrifices of children were offered to pagan deities (2 Kings 23:16). In Jesus' day it was a dump where the garbage of the city was hauled and burned. This fire burned endlessly day and night and, to the Jewish mind, was an apt depiction of the eternal fate awaiting all unbelievers.

Thus, when Jesus referred to the eternal lake of fire as *Gehenna* his listeners knew exactly what He was talking about. It was a disgusting place where the fire never stopped burning. Likewise, the real lake of fire never stops burning. Herein is the difference between *hades* and *Gehenna*. *Gehenna* is eternal, whereas *hades* is only until the final judgment. At that point, death and *hades* will be emptied into the lake of fire.

There is recognition in the world of the spirit. The rich man recognized Lazarus over in Abraham's bosom. Apparently, the spirit of man looks just like his physical body. The spirit likewise has eyes, fingers, a tongue, feelings, memory, etc. Yet it's important to realize *that we will one day be reunited with our physical bodies*. Thus, even if the spirit of man wouldn't resemble the physical body (which it clearly does), the fact that we'll again have our physical bodies shows that there will be recognition in the age to come. We'll recognize people over there just like we recognize people here. Why? Because we'll have our bodies back.

When God created man in the garden of Eden those many years ago, He created man spirit, soul, and body. Man, without his body, is not all that God intended for him to be. Those who have died are awaiting the resurrection of their bodies. For the redeemed it will be a marvelous reunion. Actually, the redeemed are going to have a *glorified* body (1 Corinthians 15:35-58), a body that cannot be touched by sickness, disease, or any limitation of this physical world. We get a glimpse of what our glorified bodies will be like when, after the resurrection in his glorified body, Jesus was still able to eat food (Luke 24:41-43) yet also pass through walls (John 20:19,26), as well as travel back and forth between the spirit world and this natural world. Our glorified bodies will also be eternally youthful — no baldness, no wrinkles, no age spots, etc. For example, the angel at the tomb after the resurrection, though many thousands of years old, appeared to be a young man (Mark 16:5). What an awesome day that is going to be.

However, for the unsaved, their reunion with their physical body is not necessarily something they're looking forward to. Why would they? Their suffering won't be any less, their future not any better, and instead of existing in the intermediary dwelling place, *hades*, they're moving to the permanent dwelling place, the lake of fire. Spirit, soul, *and body* will exist forever separated from God in *Gehenna*, the lake of fire (Matthew 10:28, Mark 5:29).

Though we can't be dogmatic, it makes sense that *Gehenna*, the lake of fire, will be worse than *hades*. To use our county jail/penitentiary analogy again, though both are prison confinements, the penitentiary is far worse than the county jail. We would think that the suffering of the spirit, soul, *and body* in *Gehenna* will be far worse than just the spirit and soul, without the body, in *hades*. Thus, the redeemed spirits in heaven's paradise are looking forward to their reunion with their bodies, whereas the unredeemed spirits in *hades* are dreading their reunion with their bodies. One group's blessings will be heightened, the other group's damnation will be deepened.

CHAPTER 9

The Fire of Hell

...for I am tormented in this FLAME.
- Luke 16:24

For a FIRE is kindled in mine anger, and shall burn unto the lowest hell...
- Deuteronomy 32:22

Fire is the one word the Bible continually uses to describe the torment of hell. Fire evokes images of the ultimate form of pain. To be burned, even if it's just an arm or leg, is the ultimate horror, let alone if it's the whole body and face. I've seen people whose whole bodies were engulfed in flames through the mishandling of gasoline around an open fire. Their suffering was inconceivable. Only the person who has experienced such a nightmare can fully understand the scope of that suffering. Nevertheless, such physical pain, as horrific as it is, is at least only temporary.

What is worse would be to experience the flame with its resultant pain on an *unending* basis. Imagine that the fire would never burn out, that the body would never burn up, and that the pain would never cease. On earth people who are seriously burned can at least die to escape the inferno. In hell dying cannot take place. Suicide isn't an option. There is no way to escape the never-ending fire.

It's interesting how some people try to dilute what the Bible actually reveals about hell. Obviously, they are hoping that hell won't be as bad as what the Bible teaches. They want to believe the Bible's description of hell is worse than what it really is. The truth is, *hell is actually worse than its description.*

For example, when people experience the death of a young child, or an unwanted divorce, or the loss of a job, no matter how descriptive their explanation, the listener will never fully understand the other's emotional devastation unless they, too, experience such a loss. Words can never convey the depths of the heartache and emotional trauma. How can we really understand the physical and emotional torture the Jew experienced during the Holocaust? How can we really understand the mental anguish of a mother whose 4 year old child has been missing for three weeks? How can we really understand what is in the mind of the person walking out of the doctor's office who has just been told he has cancer?

Words are the best we have to communicate our innermost thoughts and feelings, but they fall so very short of what we are actually experiencing. We try to explain to friends what we're going through, but we can tell by the expression on their faces they're not truly comprehending what we're saying.

Have you ever had a nightmare that you tried to describe to a friend? To you it was horrible and gut-wrenching, but as you told it to your friend, they couldn't help but smile. To you it was real. To them, though, it was amusing. Why? Because your words weren't strong enough to explain the "reality" of what you experienced.

I've had people tell me about a ride on a particular roller coaster at an amusement park. They told me about the hair-raising 210-foot drop. They described the incredible fast speeds this roller coaster attained as it went around the track. They talked about the sharp turns, the loopety-loops, the quick stops, the blazing starts. They raised their voice as they talked, used their hands, and contorted their body as they tried to help me understand how wild of a ride it was.

As good as their explanation was, though, it didn't come close to what I experienced when I finally rode the roller coaster myself. The speeds seemed faster, the drops seemed higher, and the ride seemed much wilder. Yes, I understood what they had said, but I couldn't *fully* comprehend what they had meant until I was actually on it. Words were the next best thing, but experiencing the roller coaster *personally* is what allowed me to grasp what they had been trying to say all along.

Likewise, the Bible gives us many, many warnings and depictions of hell. However, as powerful as these word pictures are, they can't fully explain the utter hopelessness and torment experienced by those already in hell. *Hell is far worse than any word description.* The fire is actually hotter, the torment worse, and the pain indescribable. No matter how excellent our mental picture of hell is, it falls far short of what is actually experienced in hell.

Is It A Real Fire?

...for I am tormented in this flame.

- Luke 16:24

Some try to explain away the fire of hell, to make it sound as if there is no fire in hell. Some have tried to compare hell's fire to a lust or passion that could never be fulfilled, as if that would be the worst punishment anyone could suffer. Certainly an eternal, unfulfilled lust or passion would be extremely difficult to deal with, if not impossible to handle, and surely that will be a part of hell. No doubt, any and all desires will never be able to be consummated, but to compare that to the fire of hell is disrespectful to the direct statement of the scriptures. The Bible is very plain about the fact that hell is full of fire.

This man referred to in Luke 16:24 plainly said that he was being tormented in a *flame*. He didn't say that he was being tormented by memories of his life back on earth. He didn't say that he was being tormented with unfulfilled passions. He didn't say he was being tormented by the fact that he didn't live for God while on earth.

Certainly he had bitter memories, unfulfilled passions, and regretted that he hadn't lived for God while on earth but, clearly, he wasn't being tormented by something other than fire here. If words mean anything at all, in his anguish, he could have cared less about using metaphors. He was in

82

torment *because of an actual fire*. He was crying out because of pain. Lest there be any doubt, notice:

And he CRIED and said, Father Abraham, have mercy on me, and send Lazarus, THAT HE MAY DIP THE TIP OF HIS FINGER IN WATER, AND COOL MY TONGUE; for I am tormented in this flame.
                                                          - Luke 16:24

If the fire of hell was just an unfulfilled lust, passion, or bitter memory he wouldn't have needed his tongue to be cooled *by water*. What good would water do for a lust, passion, or memory? Why would a drop of water on his tongue be necessary to deal with past memories or passions? Understand this, we can't take images in the Bible meant to be symbolic and call them literal, *but neither can we take images clearly literal and call them symbolic!*

Without a doubt, the flame this man was experiencing was producing the kind of torment that only water could alleviate. This man was being tormented by a fire to such a degree he was desperately in want of even a single drop of water to obtain the smallest relief. He was hoping for his tongue *to be cooled*. For something to be cooled, obviously it must be hot. If it was only his mind being tormented with lusts, passions, and memories, he wouldn't have been begging for his *tongue* to be cooled.

If we deny the scripture's description of hell, we would likewise have to deny the scripture's description of heaven. How can we say there are streets of gold in heaven and not say there is a fire in hell? If we say the fire is not fire, how can we be sure the gold is gold? In other words, we can't accept the Bible's description of heaven and deny the Bible's description of hell. To accept one part of the Bible without accepting another part of the Bible is foolish, illogical, and disrespectful to God. That is paramount to accepting the parts of the Bible that refer to the love of God, yet ignoring other parts of the Bible that refer to the severity of God (Romans 11:22) which, unfortunately, many do. However, it's inconsistent to accept one part without accepting the other part.

Some argue that a physical fire couldn't or wouldn't have any harmful effect on the spirit of man. These people fail to understand the world of the spirit. In heaven, which is in the world of the spirit, there are trees, fruit to eat from the trees, water, flowers, clothes for people to wear, houses, streets, etc. In the next life, as in this life, we'll wear clothes, drink water, eat food, live in houses, and walk on streets (see page 50). The world of the spirit is no less real than this natural world.

Likewise, if the Bible states there is fire in the next world, we can be assured that there is fire over there that is every bit as real as the fire here. If fire causes pain here it will cause pain there. The only difference is that in this world fire destroys whatever it touches, over there the fire won't destroy the spiritual body. It will cause similar pain without consuming the body it touches.

To further describe the torment associated with hell, notice:

And shall cast them into the furnace of fire: there shall be (weeping), wailing and gnashing of teeth.
- Matthew 8:12, 13:50

This confirms that the pain in hell must be far more than an unfulfilled lust. This pain results in hell's inhabitants weeping, yet not just weeping, but *wailing*. The screams in hell are long, bitter, and drawn out. They are more than moans and groans. They are the kind that come from the heart — gut-wrenching screams.

Even then, there is more to this torment than weeping and wailing, there is the *gnashing of teeth*. This shows that the pain must be intense and long. Quick, sharp pains produce screams, but not gnashing of teeth. Gnashing of teeth is the result of a horrendous, *unrelenting* pain, a kind of pain that, on earth, would make one go mad.

Hell's inhabitants are doing more than longing for their old life on earth. They're having to deal with a pain from which there is never a respite. Every nerve is pulsating with pain. Every appendage is crying for a reprieve. Every memory wishes for 5 more minutes on earth to make a heart-change decision for Christ. Yet every inhabitant knows it will never be. This is a nightmare from which there is no waking.

CHAPTER 10

More About The Fire
(The Gehenna Fire Is Eternal)

And they shall go forth, and look upon the carcases of the men that have transgressed against me: for their worm shall not die, neither shall their fire be quenched;
- Isaiah 66:24

It must be emphasized again and again the dreaded torment of hell. The scriptures are not entirely silent on the matter, yet neither do they give us as much information as we would prefer. By design God has given us as much information as is needed. He has purposely placed pieces of information in His Word here and there and, for the person who will study, he can gain a clearer picture of hell's torment. For people to think that with enough will power or stamina hell can somehow be "managed" borders on the imbecilic. There is nothing manageable about hell or what is in hell.

Spiritual suffering is difficult to describe, simply because we don't have anything with which to adequately compare it. The word "fire" is the best we have, yet people, when they think of objects being burned up, have mental pictures of things being totally annihilated. In other words, yes, the fire of hell must be horrible and the pain wretched, but in their minds they're thinking that at least it will be over in just a matter of a few minutes. This is a serious mistake.

On earth people may pass out from the trauma and shock of the flame to escape the suffering before they die, but in the lake of fire people don't die and the fire never stops. Both are eternal. Perhaps it's important to emphasize that every person ever born is going to live forever. Again, there isn't such a thing as cessation of existence. The issue is *where* they are going to spend their forever.

There are two erroneous views that need to be addressed — 1) that all wicked will one day be completely and totally annihilated and, 2) the lake of fire, the *Gehenna*-fire, will one day come to an end and all will be reconciled to God. Let's examine these.

Error 1) The wicked will be annihilated in the lake of fire.

Those who propagate this view turn to such scriptures as the following:

And fear not them which kill the body, but are not able to kill the soul; but rather fear him which is able to *destroy* both soul and body in hell (*Gehenna*).
- Matthew 10:28

In their thinking, something that is destroyed no

longer exists, therefore the soul and body of the wicked will no longer exist once they are cast into *Gehenna*. Their mistake is in their interpretation of the word "destroy." Something that is destroyed doesn't mean that it is consumed.

The Greek word translated "destroy" is *apollumi*. *Apollumi*, according to Thayer's *Greek-English Lexicon*, simply means, *"to be delivered up to eternal misery." **Never**, in any use of the word in the New Testament, does it mean to annihilate or bring to extinction or to cease to exist.

I remember a number of years ago driving through a certain area of California after an earthquake. Houses, buildings, and highways had been destroyed by the shifting of the tectonic plates beneath the surface. This didn't mean, though, that the houses, buildings, and highways that had been destroyed ceased to exist. All the essential elements and materials were still present at the site. Obviously, the original use of the materials was no longer in its intended form, but they were not annihilated. Likewise, the person cast into the lake of fire, though not in the form God originally intended them to be, still exists.

Even on earth objects and bodies that appear to be annihilated by fire are really not annihilated. Any high school science experiment will prove this to be true. For example, in one experiment a tree limb was burned. When the ashes and gases that had passed off from the limb in the fire were weighed, it turned out that nothing had been eliminated, *only the **form** of the materials had changed*. The ash and gas after the fire weighed the exact same as the limb before the fire. The point is, matter and energy cannot be annihilated!

Likewise, those cast into the lake of fire are not annihilated, they are just in an eternal "diseased" state instead of an eternal "glorified" state.

A perfect scripture to dispel the notion of the annihilation of the wicked is found in Revelation 19:20 and 20:10 when the beast and false prophet, two diabolical and demon possessed individuals, are thrown into the lake of fire:

And the beast was taken, and with him the false prophet ... These both were cast alive into a lake of fire burning with brimstone.
- Revelation 19:20

Then *1,000 years later*, after the millennium, when Satan is likewise cast into the lake of fire we see that the beast and false prophet are still existing:

And the devil that deceived them was cast into the lake of fire and brimstone, WHERE THE BEAST AND FALSE PROPHET ARE, and shall be tormented day and night forever and ever.
- Revelation 20:10

This is very clear — the beast and false prophet were not annihilated when they were cast into the lake of fire. One thousand years after they were thrown into the lake of fire *we still find them in a conscience state*. Further scriptural proof is found in Revelation 14:10-11:

...shall be tormented with fire and brimstone in the presence of the holy angels and in the presence of the

Lamb. And the smoke of their torment goes up FOREVER AND EVER; AND THEY HAVE NO REST DAY AND NIGHT, those who worship the beast and his image, and whoever receives the mark of his name.
- Revelation 14:10-11

Contrary to ceasing to exist in the lake of fire, we see that the wicked are in conscience torment *day and night forever and ever*. The wording of the scripture is quite plain. The unbeliever can't hide behind the misinterpretation of a word or phrase. For those existing in the lake of fire there isn't such a thing as rest, comfort, or annihilation. Not only is the lake of fire eternal, the inhabitants existing there are *eternal*. In conclusion, to the person with an open mind, annihilationism is not supported in the scriptures. If people choose not to believe the scriptures, then nothing will convince them otherwise until they, too, are cast into the lake of fire.

Error 2) The lake of fire will come to an end and all will be reconciled unto God.

Those who cling to this thinking that all will be saved are building their doctrine on a shallow interpretation of certain scriptures. Instead of interpreting their doctrine within the context of *all* the revealed Word of God, they take certain verses and *isolate them* from the rest of the scriptures to mean something other than what the *whole* of the scriptures teach. One of their favorite verses they, universalists, rely upon is as follows:

As in Adam all die, so also in Christ *all shall be*

made alive.

- 1 Corinthians 15:22

Unfortunately, they completely overlook other scriptures that repudiate what they try to make this verse say. For example, Jesus states in Mark 16:15-16, *"Go ye into all the world, and preach the gospel to every creature. He that believeth and is baptized shall be saved; but **he that believeth not shall be damned**."* In other words, because of Christ and what He did, it is the will of God that all be made alive unto God. However, man still has a choice in whether or not he wants to believe. If he chooses not to believe, Jesus is very clear about the fact that he will be damned. We cannot do away with Mark 16:15-16 to justify 1 Corinthians 15:22. 1 Corinthians 15:22 should be interpreted within the framework of Mark 16:15-16. Yes, in Adam all men die, but in Christ all shall be made alive *to those who will believe on Christ*.

If this doctrine, universalism, were true there would be no need to preach Christ. I mean, if all are going to be saved, what does it matter what anyone does. Why bother to exhaust one's resources and energy for something that is going to happen regardless of what we do or not do. Why be obedient to God if we can be disobedient and still go to heaven? Really, in a nutshell, universalists are saying there is no reward for obedience and there is no punishment for disobedience. Everything is going to wash out in the end. However, *Jesus contradicted this in his teaching*. Speaking of the unpardonable sin in Matthew 12:32 He said:

It shall not be forgiven him, either in this age, OR IN THE AGE TO COME.

To say that in the age to come all shall be forgiven is to completely disregard the direct statements of Jesus on the issue.

...NOW is the ACCEPTED time; behold, NOW is the day of salvation.

- 2 Corinthians 6:2

The time for people to respond to God's gift of salvation is now *in this age*, not in some future age. There is not any other accepted time. To think that we can ignore God's accepted time and hope for something different in a future age is contrary to the teaching of the scriptures. The word "accepted" means, *"to give approval to."* In other words, the only time for salvation that is approved by *God* is the time that *He* has set, which is in this *present* age, *not in the age to come*. We have to let God set the rules.

In addition, the word "all" must be understood within the context of the passage and other similar scriptures. For example, in Luke 2:1 it states that Caesar Augustus decreed that, *"all the world* should be taxed." The disciples of John the Baptist said, *"all men* come to him" (John 3:26). Matthew 3:5-6 states that, *"all* Judea" were baptized of John.

Actually, this means that the taxes were to be taken of all the world *relative to the Roman Empire*, not in the remote parts of the earth such as, say, Madagascar. Secondly, *All* hadn't come to Jesus, for the scriptures are also plain that the Pharisees and Sadducees had rejected him. Likewise, with John the Baptist, certain religious leaders in Judea didn't recognize the Baptist's ministry.

"All" in these cases doesn't mean "all" in the strictest *literal* sense of the word, but in the descriptive *figurative* sense within the context of the sentence. We, too, say similar things such as, "*Everyone* was at the party," or, "The *whole city* was at the football game," or, "*Anyone* who was anyone was there." What we mean is that there were a lot of people present, a huge crowd, perhaps the greater majority of the people in that town or city.

The word "all" in 1 Corinthians 15:22 should be understood within this framework. It is the will of God for all to be saved, but the scripture *also* says, "*whosoever shall call on the name of the Lord shall be saved*" (Acts 2:21). In other words, because it is the will of God for all to be saved, what we have to do to be saved is to call on the name of the Lord. You notice, though, that for salvation to take place *we* must do the calling. Without our calling upon Him, salvation won't take place, even though it is God's will for all to be saved.

The Fire is Eternal

Then shall he say unto them on the left hand, Depart from me, ye cursed, into EVERLASTING fire, prepared for the devil and his angels ... And these shall go away into EVERLASTING punishment: but the righteous into life ETERNAL.

- Matthew 25:41,46

The Greek word translated everlasting is *aionios*. The teaching of universalism says this Greek word *aionios* means "age-long," therefore this everlasting fire should be translated as an age-long fire, meaning the fire will come to an end after an age however many years that may be.

Their mistake, though, is to overlook the fact that this Greek word *aionois* is also used to describe not only the fire and punishment, but also the righteous life *in this very same passage*. Notice:

Then shall he say unto them on the left hand, Depart from me, ye cursed, into EVERLASTING (aionios) fire, prepared for the devil and his angels ... And these shall go away into EVERLASTING (aionios) punishment: but the righteous into life ETERNAL (aionios).

- Matthew 25:41,46

If in fact this Greek word meant only "age-long," we would also have to say that eternal life is not really eternal life, only an age-long life. Of course, any person who believes the Bible knows that life in the presence of God is going to be gloriously forever and ever. It will never ever come to an end. The point is, *aionios* is used to describe the eternal bliss the righteous will enjoy. Therefore, it would be incorrect to say *aionios* would mean only age-long. *Aionios* is used to describe eternal life *and* eternal punishment.

Further, *aionios* is also used to describe God! Notice:

But now is made manifest, and by the scriptures of the prophets, according to the commandment of the EVERLASTING (aionios) God, made known to all the nations for the obedience of faith.

- Romans 16:26

We certainly know that God is not age-lasting, He is *ever*lasting. God has always existed and always will. Therefore, *without any doubt,* **aionios means everlasting**!! God is everlasting, the life that Jesus provided through his death, burial, and resurrection for us who believe is everlasting, and the punishment and fire for the wicked is everlasting. To say that *aionios* means only age-long falls way short for any serious Bible study. Looking briefly at the few verses just mentioned we already see the error in their definition. This is the point that must again be reiterated — to understand *any* Bible truth we must allow the Bible to interpret itself. The apostle Paul said it this way, *"In the mouth of two or three (scriptural) witnesses let every word be established"* (2 Corinthians 13:1). Doctrine cannot be built upon scriptures isolated from other scriptures.

In conclusion, the lake of fire is terrifyingly forever. The exact same Greek word used to describe the duration of God is used to describe the duration of the *Gehenna*-fire. The lake of fire does *not* come to an end and the torment of its inhabitants does *not* come to an end. There is no redemption for the unsaved except in this life. The Bible doctrine of eternal judgment is just that — *eternal* judgment. To hope that God will change his mind after eons of time have elapsed has no foundation in the Bible.

CHAPTER
11

Degrees Of Judgment

Woe unto thee, Chorazin! Woe unto thee, Bethsaida! for if the mighty works, which were done in you, had been done in Tyre and Sidon they would have repented long ago in sackcloth and ashes. But I say unto you, it shall be MORE TOLERABLE for Tyre and Sidon AT THE DAY OF JUDGMENT, THAN FOR YOU.
                                        - Matthew 11:21-22

Just as there are varying degrees of rewards for the righteous in heaven there are varying degrees of judgment for the unrighteous in hell. According to Jesus, it's going to be *more tolerable* in hell for some than for others. The fact that it's going to be more tolerable for some people shows that the suffering of some is going to be much worse than the suffering of others. This is a sobering thought worth considering. As horrendous as it is for anyone to be in hell, there are some whose torment will be more acute.

Eternal death can be compared to the diseased on earth. Though all cancer is bad, the suffering of some cancers is worse than the suffering of other cancers. Or, within the same category of cancer, the suffering of the final stages is worse than the earlier stages. Generally, the farther into the body the cancer has spread, the worse the physical suffering will be.

So it is with those suffering from eternal death. The more debauched and raucous the sin, the worse the spiritual nature degrades. The grosser the wickedness the unsaved yield themselves to, the more the spiritual nature declines. Clearly, sin is a disease. The further to sin the sinner opens his heart, the worse his spiritual condition succumbs to the disease.

As a result, when he crosses to the other side of the grave, the more debased his spiritual condition is, the more pronounced his suffering will be. Again, it's the sinner's *condition* that is the cause of his torment. The farther the sin has progressed, similar to the farther a physical disease has progressed in the body, the more severe the suffering.

Generally speaking, the suffering of those in hell is linked to the condition of their spiritual nature. Because the unsaved have not been born again, their spirit is dead to God. Without the life of God in it, it couldn't be anything but dead. Thus, when they leave their physical body their nature is free to manifest its "deadness," and their suffering immediately begins upon physical death. But it is the condition of their spirit that is the cause of their excruciating torment, not God.

God didn't want them to go into eternity in that dead condition, which is why God sent Jesus to his death, burial, and resurrection. His victory over death cleared the way for all human spirits to once again have the life of God in them. The miracle of the new birth is just that — a miracle. Yet when the sinner rejects the lordship of Jesus, he keeps God from doing what He wants to do in his life. God will not "make" people do what they don't want to do. If people prefer darkness over light God allows them their prerogative. As a result, they cross the grave in their diseased condition and suffer the consequences of who and what they are.

The *Judgment* of Hell

There is another aspect to hell that is likewise sobering — judgment. There are some classes of people that take sin to extraordinary depths. They use their sin as a springboard to intrude into the lives of others and inflict pain.

For example, Hitler didn't just exist in this world as a sinner, but he used whatever abilities he possessed to foster hate and fear to destroy the lives of others. With his power, instead of using it for good, he used it for evil purposes. How many untold millions, because of him, suffered emotionally, were tortured physically, and died cruel and inhumane deaths? Yes, he's suffering in hell because of his diseased spiritual condition, but he's also suffering in *judgment from God* for his perverted misuse of power in destroying the innocent.

Further, what about those who molest children? Who through such twisted actions emotionally destroy innocent children. What about those who kidnap children and torture them physically, eventually killing many of them with horrible methods? What about serial killers? Rapists?

These disgusting people are not only sinners, they're using their occasion of sin *to violate others*. It's one thing to sin, it's another thing to harm others. Their hell is going to be on a different scale than others. We get a glimpse of this in the Old Testament:

For a fire is kindled in mine anger, and shall burn unto the LOWEST hell...

- Deuteronomy 32:22

If there is a *lowest* hell, it makes sense that there is a *highest* hell. We can assume then that there are levels in between the lowest and highest levels, with the lowest level being the worst torment imaginable. In this level we might find the Hitlers, the Stalins, and the most degraded individuals who walked the earth. These might be the ones who purposely destroyed others for their selfish gain or perverted pleasure. These might be ones who delighted in seeing the pain and anguish on the faces of those they were mutilating, gleefully watching them taking their last breaths. It's difficult to describe the wretchedness of certain individuals who willingly open their hearts and minds to demonic influence and persuasion.

We also see that the lowest part of hell is associated with God's anger:

For a fire is kindled in MINE ANGER, and shall burn unto the lowest hell...

Woe unto them who live such wicked lives as to draw the anger of God. In this lowest section of hell where the fire seems to be stoked because of God's fury are those who were rightly judged for the unrestrained evil they inflicted on others. Sadly, there are many more yet to enter this section of hell. A brief scan of any newspaper reveals the hideous acts of too many individuals and groups, and this list seems to be growing with more and more masochists and perverts every day. We see isolated individuals, groups of terrorists, and a number of dictators getting by with too many hate crimes upon multiplied tens of thousands.

Yet all is being recorded in books that will one day be opened. Nothing is being overlooked by God. Every unsaved person will one day face a day of fearful reckoning for what they did:

And I saw the dead, the great and the small, standing before the throne, and books were opened; and another book was opened, which is the book of life; *and the dead were judged from the things which were written in the books, ACCORDING TO THEIR DEEDS.*
- Revelation 20:12

This confirms that the unsaved will be judged differently from each other. Their basis of judgement will be in accordance with what they did on earth. The degree of punishment will exactly fit the offence. This is staggering to consider. No one will be able to hide behind an unjust attorney. No one will be able to pay off an unjust judge. No loopholes, no appeals, just the plain, irrefutable, documented facts. No one will be able to say, *"I didn't mean to do that,"* because even the hidden thoughts and motives will be exposed. Nothing will be misinterpreted, for everything will be displayed with perfect analysis.

We get further insight into the different degrees of judgment from the words of Jesus:

And that servant, which knew his lord's will, and prepared not himself, neither did according to his will, shall be beaten with MANY stripes. But he that knew not, and did commit things worthy of stripes, shall be beaten with FEW stripes. For unto whomsoever much is given, of him shall be much required...

- Luke 12:47-48

Whether their judgment is with many stripes or few stripes is based on how they respond with what they know. Everyone has a conscience. Unfortunately, some consciences are seared worse than others. The more we disregard our conscience, the less we're able to hear it when it again speaks until eventually we can't hear it at all. When we fail to take heed to our conscience it becomes sin to us.

Therefore to him that knoweth to do good, and doeth it not, to him it is sin.

- James 4:17

The more we know the more we are held accountable. To whom much is given much is required. If we've been taught scriptural truths or if we've been taught right from wrong, if we go against what we know, our judgment will be more severe than for someone who may have committed the same sin but hadn't been taught that it was wrong. The more seared the conscience, the more depraved the sin. Consequently, the greater the judgment.

Initially, a conscience is very tender. A conscience only becomes seared when it is continually ignored. The reason we ignore it is because we *want* to do what's wrong. For example, if someone is contemplating adultery there is something on the inside of them that is telling them it's wrong to do it. No matter how they try to justify it in their mind, their conscience is telling them not to. If they then decide to commit adultery they're doing it over what that "inside something" is telling them. As they continue to do things their conscience tells them not to, it will come to the point where they won't hear their conscience at all. Of course, whether or not they hear their conscience, sin is still sin. They're either overriding their conscience, or it means they've seared their conscience. People sin because they *want* to.

According to Jesus, then, some people will suffer in the next life with a greater number of stripes than others. Clearly, some will have fewer stripes. Yet hell is still hell. Don't think for one moment that it will be easy to be in the highest section of hell if, for no other reason, because of the depraved condition of the dead spirit. As noted earlier, the spirit of the unsaved suffers tremendously. The embers of the dead spirit are continually stirring the flames of torment on the inside of them. The fire never stops because that man or woman never allowed the Spirit of God to impart life to their spirit. *Their spirit is malignant.*

The knowledge we've been exposed to is the measuring stick by how everyone will be judged:

Woe unto thee, Chorazin! Woe unto thee, Bethsaida! for if the mighty works, which were done in you, had been done in Tyre and Sidon they would have repented long ago in sackcloth and ashes. But I say unto you, it shall be more tolerable for Tyre and Sidon at the day of judgment, than for you.

And thou, Capernaum, which art exalted unto heaven, shalt be brought down to hell: FOR IF THE MIGHTY WORKS, WHICH HAVE BEEN DONE IN THEE, HAD BEEN DONE IN SODOM, IT WOULD HAVE REMAINED UNTIL THIS DAY. But I say unto you, That it shall be more tolerable for the land of Sodom in the day of judgment, than for thee.

- Matthew 11:21-24

If Sodom had witnessed the same miracles that Capernaum had witnessed under the ministry of Jesus they would have repented! In other words, because less knowledge had been imparted to Sodom, their judgment won't be as severe as what the unbelievers in Capernaum will experience.

Capernaum had been exposed to the most supernatural ministry the earth had ever been exposed to. They had witnessed the most amazing miracles anyone had ever seen. They had heard the easiest-to-understand Bible teaching anyone could have ever heard. Yet they opted to not believe in Jesus. Therefore, because they denied what God considered to be infallible proofs, *which even Sodom would have believed*, Capernaum's judgment in the next life will be worse than Sodom's.

The point is, because everyone doesn't have the same opportunity to receive equal Bible knowledge, everyone won't be judged by the same measuring stick. People will be judged by the scriptural information and spiritual manifestations that had been made available to their generation. This is why people in countries such as the United States will face a much severer judgment than the people living in, say, Timbuktu. From its founding days the United States has consistently had a godly influence sustained within its borders. If certain people in the United States choose not to live for God, they are knowingly trampling over the blood of Jesus and all He stands for. To say this minister failed or that minister failed is not a good enough excuse. We are held accountable for what we know, not by the failings of others.

Actually, to not live for God because of what some religious leader may have done is only a lame excuse to keep doing what one really wants to do. It's like what we facetiously ask our children, *"If so-and-so jumps off a cliff, does that mean you would jump off a cliff, too?"* If people want to do wrong, they can find as many excuses to justify their actions as there are people, because mankind will always fail. Religious leaders are still only human, too. *God's Word is what we live by*, not the lifestyles of certain people, religious or otherwise.

How much light we've been *given* is the measuring stick by how people will be judged:

...For unto whomsoever much is GIVEN, of him shall be much required.

- Luke 12:48

I think it's important to point out that this verse does not say, "For unto whomsoever much is RECEIVED, of him shall be much required." In other words, if people choose not to hear certain truths because it doesn't fit in with what they want to do, or if they don't want to take the time to understand certain truths because they think it might force them to alter their life, they're not excused. Just because people fail to comprehend what is quickened to their spirit or what is said in the pulpit doesn't mean they're not held accountable for it. If it has been *given*, it's required of us. It is *our* responsibility to examine and study what has been *given* to make the corresponding change. If we fail to understand it's not the responsibility of the one who gave it to change us. He did his part in giving it. Now it's up to us to incorporate it.

Every generation is given a certain amount of light. Obviously, some have been given more than others, but all are held accountable to the degree that they have. The rewards dispersed to believers and the judgment dealt to unbelievers is based on this fundamental truth — less light, less required. More light, more required.

CHAPTER 12

The Error of Predestination
(Does God Predestine Some to Hell?)

In whom also we have obtained an inheritance, being *predestinated* according to the purpose of him who worketh all things after the counsel of his own will:
- Ephesians 1:11

Some people have erroneously thought that they were predestined to hell while others were predestined to heaven. In other words, they thought before they were born that God, without allowing them a choice, *predetermined* where they would spend eternity. That is, God decided *for them* who would go to heaven and who would go to hell. As a result, some people have never sought God for salvation wrongly thinking there was nothing they could do to escape hell.

This doctrine is extremely dangerous because it ignores the free will of mankind. If man doesn't have a choice in spiritual matters, then yes, God would be unjust to send a person to hell. However, the truth is that man does have a choice. There are too many clear-cut scriptures for there to be any doubt in this matter. Here are just a few:

For God so loved the world, that he gave his only begotten Son, that WHOSOEVER BELIEVETH IN HIM SHOULD NOT PERISH, but have everlasting life.

- John 3:16

...WHOSOEVER shall call on the name of the Lord shall be saved.

- Acts 2:21

...WHOSOEVER BELIEVETH on him shall not be ashamed. For there is no difference between the Jew and the Greek: for the same Lord over all is rich UNTO ALL THAT CALL UPON HIM. For WHOSOEVER shall call upon the name of the Lord shall be saved.

- Romans 10:11-13

...WHOSOEVER shall confess me before men, him shall the son of man also confess before the angels of God: But he that denieth me before men shall be denied before the angels of God.

- Luke 12:8-9

...the Son of man must be lifted up: That WHOSOEVER believeth in him should not perish, but have eternal life.

- John 3:14-15

...HIM THAT COMETH TO ME I will in no wise

cast out.

- John 6:37

The Lord is...*not willing that any should perish*, but that ALL should come to repentance.

- 2 Peter 3:9

And the Spirit and the bride say, Come. And let him that heareth say, Come. And let him that is athirst come. And WHOSOEVER WILL, let him take the water of life freely.

- Revelation 22:17

There is an overwhelming number of scriptures in addition to these just mentioned that make this same point. *Whosoever* simply means *anyone* and *everyone*. Absolutely no one has to go to hell. Anyone and everyone has the same opportunity for salvation. It is simply a matter of choosing to believe on Jesus.

Predestination is a Biblical term denoting a *plan*, **not** a *person* or *persons*. It is referring to the *plan* that God has for all who will believe. God intends for everyone to be a part of this plan, but unfortunately, not everyone will be a part of it simply because they don't want to be, *not because God doesn't want them to.*

Predestinate is a word composed of two parts — 1) *pre*, meaning before and, 2) *destinate*, meaning destiny. In other words, our destiny, or we could say, *our purpose for being created* was planned by God somewhere in eternity past before there was an Adam and Eve. God had a glorious destiny for mankind, but when Adam and Eve fell, that *pre*determined destiny, that plan, was temporarily put on hold. However, Jesus came to purchase mankind back with His precious blood so that this plan could eventually be resumed. In the ages to come this predestinated plan from eternity past will unfold and be consummated.

To say that predestination means that God automatically damned certain people to hell before they were even born is not only incorrect, but absurd, even ludicrous. Again, God predestinated a plan, not a people. The apostle Paul uses this word occasionally in his letters to the churches to reveal and teach those who chose to believe in Jesus what an awesome blessing awaited those who chose to be a part of this predestinated plan. This is why we have been commanded to preach the gospel. If we can get others to see it and believe they, too, can be partakers of this plan, of which we have a marvelous inheritance.

Foreknowledge Is Not Predestination

Some have argued, *"But did not God hate Esau and love Jacob before they were born? Wouldn't this prove that God predestined Esau to a life of cursing and not blessing?"* Of course they're referring to Paul in Romans 9:13, *"As it is written, Jacob have I loved, but Esau have I hated."*

The answer is really quite simple. Because God knows the future just as clearly as He knows the past, He already knew the course in life that Esau would choose. Likewise, God already knew that Jacob, in spite of his youthful carnality, had a heart bent towards God and things spiritual.

Sadly, Esau looked at life from a perspective totally devoid of any spiritual influence. The scriptures record a number of instances of Esau's bad choices that prove this point. Hebrews 12:16 more or less sums up Esau's character:

Lest there be any fornicator, or profane person, AS ESAU, who for one morsel of meat sold his birthright.

God didn't predestine Esau to be the way he was, he *foreknew* Esau would be that way. In other words, Esau *chose* to be the way he was, and because God knows the beginning from the end he saw Esau's life choices before he was born. Based upon this knowledge God chose Jacob over Esau.

Also, the word "hate" here in the *King James Version* is misleading. God didn't *hate* Esau in the way that people today use this word. Lest there be any doubt about this, Luke 14:26 in the KJV illustrates this very well, *"If any man come to me, and **hate** not his father, and mother, and wife, and children, and brethren, and sisters, yea, and his own life also, he cannot be my disciple."*

There is not any person who chose to *hate* their family in order to become a Christian. Actually, *just the opposite is taught in the scriptures.* For example, 1 John 2:11 says, *"he that hateth his brother is in darkness,"* and 1 John 3:14 says, *"We know that we have passed from death unto life, because we love the brethren. He that loveth not his brother abideth in death."* The point is, we don't hate others to get saved, *we just choose to love God more than we love others.*

The word "hate" in Luke 14:26 and Romans 9:13

should more accurately be understood as a *preference*. We *prefer* Christ over our friends and loved ones. Likewise, God *preferred* Jacob over Esau because He knew the dastardly direction Esau would choose in life.

When we discuss God's foreknowledge we're wading into deep waters. Yes, God already knows everyone who will go to hell. The mistake people make, though, is to assume that because God knows the direction people will choose He then gives up on them before they even have a chance. Nothing could be further from the truth. Look at Cain and Abel for example. God obviously foreknew that Cain would one day murder his brother Abel. Nevertheless, God took the time to warn him:

And the Lord said unto Cain, Why art thou wroth? And why is thy countenance fallen? If thou doest well, shalt thou not be accepted? And if thou doest not well, sin lieth at the door...

- Genesis 4:6-7

God deals with *every* man for salvation because God is just and fair. Acts 10:34 says that God is not a respecter of persons. God shows no partiality concerning salvation. Every person has an equal opportunity. *God sees to it that they have the opportunity.* However, in the face of equal opportunity for salvation, God already knows which ones will believe and which ones won't.

People then say, "But if God knows what decision I'll make then there's nothing I can do to change it." This is where they are wrong. They can do anything they want because, ultimately, they are the makers of their own destiny. Just because God knew that Cain would murder Abel it didn't mean that Cain had no choice in the matter. The murder was *Cain's* decision, not God's. God only knew he would do it. Likewise, just because God knows what decision you'll make for salvation, it doesn't mean you're not fully accountable for your own decision. God doesn't *make* you get saved.

Further, hell (*Gehenna*) wasn't even made for man in the first place. According to Matthew 25:41 *Gehenna* was prepared for Satan and his angels. This is a direct statement of *Jesus*. So if God was going to predestine some people to go to *Gehenna*, Jesus would have had to say that the lake of fire was made for Satan, the fallen angels, *and those men whom God wanted to go there*. This He did not say. Clearly, then, man was never predestinated to go to the lake of fire *according to Jesus* in Matthew 25:41. Mankind was predestinated for eternal fellowship with God. *Gehenna* was specifically created by God for Satan and his angels, not man.

Why then do people go to hell (*hades*) and, ultimately, to *Gehenna*? Because some people don't want to have anything to do with God and his predestinated plan. Therefore, hell was enlarged to take in those people who prefer iniquity over salvation. Did God *foreknow* their decision? Yes. Did God *control* their decision? **No**. Actually, God did everything within his means to persuade them to choose salvation over damnation, not vice-versa.

The Power of Free Will

...And WHOSOEVER WILL, let him take the

113

water of life freely.

- Revelation 22:17

Everyone has the power to will what they want in life. The fact that man has the ability to resist moral sin shows the person with an open mind that man has the will power to do that which is right or wrong. No one is *forced* by God to do right just as no one is *forced* by God to do wrong. Man may *know* what is right and wrong, but the ultimate decision on what he does is left with *him*.

There are a number of scriptures that prove this point. Here are just a few:

...CHOOSE you this day whom ye will serve:
- Joshua 24:15

...they have CHOSEN their own ways...
- Isaiah 66:3

I have CHOSEN the way of truth:
- Psalm 119:30

...if I do this thing WILLINGLY...
- 1 Corinthians 9:17

...hath power over HIS OWN WILL...
- 1 Corinthians 7:37

Man has the ability to *choose* what he wants, what he does, where he goes, how he gets there, and who he wants to be with. Joshua made it very plain that whom we serve is up to our choosing. The word *choose* proves the free will of man, for if man does not have a free will there wouldn't be any choices to be made. All decisions would be made for us.

Further, the fact that we have been commanded by Jesus to preach the gospel to the whole world so that people can believe proves the free will of man. If man doesn't have a free will there would be no need to preach, for everyone's eternal decision would be made for them. I mean, why preach if there's no need to preach? Why give people the opportunity to believe if there's no opportunity to be taken advantage of? It's a complete waste of time and effort.

In addition, the fact that some people say we don't have a free will while others say we do have a free will proves mankind's free will. If mankind doesn't have a free will there wouldn't be two opposing views on this matter. All would be forced to believe only one thing. Yet the obvious fact of so many different churches believing many diverse doctrines further proves our free will.

Man is not a robot programmed to do only one thing. Men and women are complex beings with a host of decisions confronting them every day — *"Should I wear yellow socks or red? Should I wear dress pants or jeans? Do I want to go to bed early or stay up late? Do I want a haircut or grow my hair long? Do I want to go to church or stay home? Do I want to live for God or live for me? Do I want to fulfill God's plan for my life or do what I want to do?"*

We have a choice in how we are going to live our lives. The fact that Adam ate of the forbidden tree against

God's strictest order likewise proves our free will. Notice:

But of the tree of the knowledge of good and evil, *thou shalt not eat of it...*

- Genesis 2:17

...and (she) gave also unto her husband with her; *and he did eat.*

- Genesis 3:6

Here we have as clear a picture as the scriptures give. This is not just talking about physical death, though certainly physical death was a part of this, but this is talking about spiritual death. These are matters with eternal ramifications. God did not *force* Adam to eat of the tree of the knowledge of good and evil, and neither did God *keep* Adam from eating of the tree of the knowledge of good and evil. God *told* Adam what to do and what not to do. Adam's actions were his own decisions.

If there ever would have been a time for God to control someone's destiny this would have been that time. Yet God stepped back and let Adam choose his own destiny. God didn't choose Adam and Eve's destiny, *they* did. God had a predestinated plan for them, but *they* chose another path. As a result, we are still reaping the consequences today of what they chose then.

Mankind has a will free to choose what *they* want. The apostle Paul plainly said that we have the power over our own will (1 Corinthians 9:17). The decisions we make rest on our shoulders and no one else's. We certainly have a moral obligation to live a godly lifestyle, yet no one is forced to live it if they don't will to. God has predestinated a glorious eternity for all, but where we go is up to us. Man has a free will to choose his moral decisions, his physical life decisions, and his spiritual life decisions.

CHAPTER
13

What About Those Who Never Heard About Jesus?

...Shall not the Judge of all the earth do right?
- Genesis 18:25

And that servant, which knew his lord's will, and prepared not himself, neither did according to his will, shall be beaten with many stripes.

But he that knew not, and did commit things worthy of stripes, shall be beaten with few stripes. FOR UNTO WHOMSOEVER MUCH IS GIVEN, OF HIM SHALL BE MUCH REQUIRED: and to whom men have committed much, of him they will ask the more.
- Luke 12:47-48

When we discuss salvation and the consequences of those who refuse to believe, sooner or later the question has to be answered about all the people who have *not* heard about Jesus. Do they go to hell? Will they spend their eternity separated from God? Are they doomed simply because of logistics, over which they had no control, about where they were born?

This further leads into questions about babies that die. Do babies that die go to heaven? Or do they go to hell? Are they doomed simply because they didn't have the opportunity to grow up to hear about Jesus?

Let's discuss first from the scriptures about babies. David made a revealing statement concerning the death of his own child:

But now he is dead, wherefore should I fast? Can I bring him back again? I SHALL GO TO HIM, BUT HE SHALL NOT RETURN TO ME.

- 2 Samuel 12:23

David had a baby that died 7 days after its birth. When David was informed by his servants about the infant's death, he got up from his mourning, cleaned, and changed his clothes. He realized his baby would not be able to come back to life to be with him, but he acknowledged that the day would come in the afterlife *when he would join his child.* Since David is obviously not in hell, but is presently in heaven, HIS CHILD IS CLEARLY IN HEAVEN ALSO.

We see, then, that when children die, they don't go to hell, they go to heaven. There is not one child who died prematurely that went to hell. *There are no children in hell!* Conversely, heaven is full of children. In heaven we'll hear children giggling, teasing, and playing. To say that there are no children in heaven is ludicrous and unscriptural.

Jesus further stated that for one to go to heaven he had to become like a little child:

Suffer the little children to come unto me, and forbid them not: FOR OF SUCH IS THE KINGDOM OF GOD.

- Mark 10:14

Verily I say unto you, Except ye be converted, AND BECOME AS LITTLE CHILDREN, ye shall not enter into the kingdom of heaven.

- Matthew 18:3

Clearly, the kingdom of God is composed of little children. Jesus welcomed little children to come to him. When the disciples tried to keep certain children away from him, He rebuked the disciples. He said that children were a part of God's kingdom. Of course, little children entering heaven don't remain little children. As on earth they eventually grow up to become young men and women. After they've grown they are able to fulfill the plan that God has for them.

It's important to realize that eternity is not going to be a time of idleness and inactivity. Actually, eternity is where productivity and accomplishment will begin to be consummated. This present earth life, because of sin, is only a brief deviation from God's ultimate purpose in creating mankind. Our present commission is to spread the gospel of the Lord Jesus Christ. Once this life, as we know it, is over is when eternity will begin. With multiplied trillions of years in front of us is when we'll finally be able to recognize God's ultimate purpose in our creation. So, yes, there will be much to accomplish in eternity.

In addition, the greater majority of children born all over the world die in infancy or early childhood. For them to hear about Jesus is not even an issue. As a result, multiplied millions of children from every nation, tribe, and tongue enter heaven. Heaven is full of children from India, Africa, China, South America, Russia, the Middle East, the Philippines, etc. All nationalities, peoples, and tongues are represented from earth in heaven. Heaven is incredibly diverse. The truth is, the adults in second and third world countries are only a small fraction of the actual number of people that were born in their respective countries. Earth will be well represented in heaven.

What About Those Who Never Heard?

It's important to realize that God is the fairest judge of all. He is more equitable in his judgments than any who have ever lived. It's hard for some to imagine that God is a Being who actually knows *everything*, but there is absolutely nothing hidden from his understanding and comprehension (Hebrews 4:13). How God knows the innermost thoughts and motives of *every* person who has ever lived is difficult to grasp. Nevertheless, that's why He is God. He sees all and knows all.

It's also important to realize that if you are reading this book you are without excuse. You *have* heard about Jesus. You know that Jesus shed his blood for our sin. If people have a television set, they, too, are without excuse, because at some time in their life they heard someone on their

TV tell them about Jesus. So to think that somehow God will be merciful to us in the afterlife if we have rejected what we've heard about Jesus is preposterous. What we're discussing now are people who truly have *never* heard the gospel preached to them *in any form or fashion*. What about them?

Paul gave us some information along this line:

For as many as have sinned without law shall also perish without law; and as many as have sinned in the law shall be judged by the law; For not the hearers of the law are just before God, but the doers of the law shall be justified. FOR WHEN THE GENTILES, WHICH HAVE NOT THE LAW, DO BY NATURE THE THINGS CONTAINED IN THE LAW, THESE HAVING NOT THE LAW, ARE A LAW UNTO THEMSELVES.
- Romans 2:12-14

In other words, people who have never heard about Jesus will be judged by the light of nature and their own conscience. Unless a person sears their own conscience there is something on the inside of him that says there is a God. What he does with that knowledge is in his hands. Sadly, many violate their conscience by ignoring that innate understanding from childhood that recognizes God. Just because we can't see God or don't hear preaching about God, it doesn't mean we're excused from believing in God and living for God to the degree that He's revealed Himself to us.

For example, if we would never see water, taste water, or feel water, we would still know there is such a thing as water. Why? Because there is something on the inside of us, inside our bodies, that says there must be water since our bodies crave it and need it to sustain life.

Further, if we would never see food, taste food, or handle food, we would still know there is such a thing as food. Why? Because there is something on the inside of us, in our bodies, that says there must be food since our bodies crave it and need it to sustain life.

The point is, just because we don't see God, we still know there is a God. Why? Because there is something on the inside of us, in our spirits, that says there must be a God since our spirits crave Him and need Him to sustain our spiritual life.

Deep down in our innermost being, our spirit calls out to the God of creation. *The truth is, man has to be taught not to believe in God.* Agnosticism and atheism hold sway only over those who prefer self-will over God's will. People who will truly and sincerely be honest with themselves will recognize there is something deep on the inside of them that acknowledges there is a God. Only a fool says in his heart there is no God (Psalm 14:1).

Just because a certain group of people proclaim themselves intelligent, cosmopolitan, and elegant, it doesn't mean they aren't fools. Actually, that should be the proof. Being a fool has nothing to do with IQ or money. There are rich fools and intelligent fools. Fools are those who fail to be brutally honest with themselves, especially so concerning spiritual matters. Fools are also those who are self-deceived into thinking they're something they're not. They are deceived because they want to be deceived. Surprisingly, many of them even go to church. Of course, their purposes are other than sincere. Usually, if it's not for political or social purposes, it's for them to look down on those they consider hypocrites so they can justify in their minds why they are the way they are.

The fact is, the creation attests to a Creator. If a person refuses to believe in God it is simply because they don't want to believe, not because the facts aren't abundantly obvious. There is a God. It is these people's love of darkness over light that is their condemnation.

And this is the condemnation, that light is come into the world, and men loved darkness rather than light, because their deeds were evil.
- John 3:19

According to Paul in Romans 2:12-14, then, if certain people don't have the written Law, they will be judged by that law which is written upon their conscience. Jesus gave us some insight along this line:

If ye were blind, ye should have no sin: but now ye say, We see; therefore your sin remaineth.
- John 9:41

According to Jesus, people are released from the penalty of their sin if they're truly blind in spiritual matters. In other words, *they can't believe in Jesus if they have never even heard the name of Jesus.* Thus, God won't judge them for failing to believe in Jesus, simply because they had never been given such an opportunity. Based upon their ignorance, their sin is not accounted to them. Jesus further said:

If I had not come and spoken unto them, they had not had sin: but now they have no cloak for their sin.
- John 15:22

The people Jesus is referring to in this passage would have had a cloak from their sin — a covering, if you will, over their sin if they would have never had Jesus come to them and preach. But because He revealed Himself to them they were held accountable. This seems to be the key upon which the future judgment will be based — *people's response to light when it comes.* To whom much is given, much is required (Luke 12:48). Not everyone is given the same amount of information, but whatever light has been given is the measuring stick by how people will be judged, good and bad.

Some people can do a lot with a little, while others fail to do a little with a lot. This is true among those who believe just as much as among those who don't. The rewards among the faithful will be passed out in accordance to the revelation given them. Some Christians through the ages accomplished an incredible work for God with very little revelation of God's Word. Yet others who had possession of our many redemptive truths accomplished very little. Rewards will be passed out accordingly.

Similarly, judgment will be dealt by God to the sinner according to the available light given in their generation. Those people who were exposed to much light will face a harsher judgment than those who had little light available to them (Matthew 11:21-24). Since, obviously, not every nation has heard about Jesus, God will deal with them in accordance with what precious little they do have. Their reaction to their conscience will be central to their eternity.

This is the beauty about the gospel of the Lord Jesus Christ *since no one lives up to all he knows*. When we fail — and we all do — Jesus wonderfully paid the penalty for our failure. This is why we should fervently preach Jesus to the world. They need a savior. The wages of sin is death, and the gift of God is eternal life.

In Conclusion

When we discuss the consequences of the uninformed we're again wading into deep waters. Suffice it to say, the judge of all the earth will do right. He won't allow one person to go to hell who, given the opportunity, would have received Jesus. When we look at the creation of the earth and our corresponding universe, in spite of the curse the world is presently under because of the fall of man, we still see the marvelous and astounding work God had in mind those many years ago when He first created. *If God's handiworks are perfect, should we think that His judgments would not be?* The truth is, we need not worry about how God will dispense justice since everything else He has done has been perfect. God will do what is fair and right, just as He will do that which is honorable.

It is my concern that some, because of their knowledge of God's love and mercy, will falsely hope for judicial leniency on the day of judgment. Yet that knowledge is why they won't get leniency — they are already aware of God's love and mercy through Jesus Christ *now*. They're ignoring God's free gift of salvation because they love darkness more than they love light. The needed light for salvation has already come to them and they're bypassing it in favor of their want for sin.

Unfortunately, though, sin only has pleasure for a season (Hebrews 11:25). Its wage is high and its collector comes suddenly without any prearranged meeting time. No one is ever ready when it unexpectedly shows up on the front steps of their life.

The mistake of so very many is to speculate endlessly with other non-believers on what they want to think about Christ's redemption instead of on what the scriptures reveal about His redemption. As Abraham said to the rich man in hell, *"They have Moses and the prophets* (God's Word), *let them hear them."* This nation and many others have been given God's Word on salvation, therefore we are without excuse. To think that everything will be okay with us spiritually because we think we're "good" people is the shallowest of thinking.

How shall we escape, if we neglect so great salvation...

- Hebrews 2:3

CHAPTER
14

AN EXTRACT OUT OF JOSEPHUS' DISCOURSE TO THE GREEKS CONCERNING HADES

I thought it might be of interest to the reader to be exposed to the writings of Flavius Josephus* (A.D. 37 - 100) concerning the subject of hell. Certainly his writings are not inspired yet nevertheless give us much insight into the Jewish mind-set during the time of Christ and the first century. Concerning our study here, what he says about the underworld corresponds very closely with what Jesus shared about hell in Luke 16:19-31.

---

* Flavius Josephus was a Jewish historian most noted for his writing *The Antiquities of the Jews*, which chronicles the
(continued bottom next page)

The Jews fully understood that both the righteous and unrighteous went to the underworld at physical death and that they were separated by a great gulf. They also believed that the righteous were in comfort and the unrighteous in torment. Of course, not believing in Jesus or his resurrection, the Jews still believed that at death they went to *hades*, not heaven. We also see their insight concerning the future resurrection. Further, they looked at those on the torment side of *hades* as suffering *temporary* punishment with the future punishment being in the lake of fire.

JOSEPHUS' DISCOURSE TO THE GREEKS CONCERNING HADES

1. Now as to Hades, wherein the souls of the righteous and unrighteous are detained, it is necessary to speak of it. Hades is a place in the world not regularly finished; a *subterraneous* region, wherein the light of this world does not shine; from which circumstance, that in this region the light does not shine, it cannot be but there must be in it perpetual *darkness*. This region is allotted as a place of custody for souls, in which angels are appointed as guardians to them, who distribute to them *temporary punishments*, agreeable to everyone's behavior and manners.

2. In this region there is a certain place set apart, as *a lake of unquenchable fire*, whereinto we suppose no one hath hitherto

---

Jewish story from the Biblical creation to the fall of Masada. In his writing he even gives brief references to Jesus, John the Baptist, and James, the brother of Jesus. Josephus was well educated and followed the Pharisaic form of Judaism.

been cast; but it is prepared for a day aforedetermined by God, in which one righteous sentence shall deservedly be passed upon all men; when the unjust and those that have been disobedient to God, and have given honor to such idols as have been the vain operations of the hands of men, as to God himself, shall be adjudged to this *everlasting punishment*, as having been the causes of defilement; while the just shall obtain *an incorruptible* and never-fading *kingdom*. These are now indeed confined in Hades, but not in the same place wherein the unjust are confined.

3. For there is one descent into this region, at whose *gate* we believe there stands an archangel with an host; which *gate* when those pass through that are conducted down by the angels appointed over souls, they do not go the same way; but the just are guided to the *right hand*, and are led with hymns, sung by the *angels* appointed over that place, unto a region of *light*, in which the just have dwelt from the beginning of the world; not constrained by necessity, but ever enjoying the prospect of the good things they see, and rejoice in the expectation of those new enjoyments, which will be peculiar to every one of them, and esteeming those things beyond what we have here; with whom there is no place of toil, no burning heat, no piercing cold, nor are any briers there; but the countenance of the *fathers* and of the just, which they see always smiles upon them while they wait for that rest and *eternal* new *life in heaven*, which is to succeed this region. This place we call *The Bosom of Abraham*.

4. But as to the unjust, they are dragged by force to the *left hand* by the angels allotted for punishment, no longer going with a good will, but as prisoners driven by violence; to whom are sent the angels appointed over them to reproach them and threaten them with their terrible looks, and to thrust them still downwards.

Now those angels that are set over these souls, drag them into the neighborhood of hell itself; who, when they are hard by it, continually hear the noise of it, and do not stand clear of the hot vapor itself; but when they have a nearer view of this spectacle, as of a terrible and exceeding great prospect of fire, they are struck with a fearful expectation of a future judgment, and in effect punished thereby: and not only so, but where they see the place [or choir] of the *fathers* and of the just, even hereby are they punished; for a *chaos* deep and large is fixed between them; insomuch that a just man that hath compassion upon them cannot be admitted, nor can one that is unjust if he were bold enough to attempt it, pass over it.

5. This is the discourse concerning Hades, wherein the souls of all men are confined until a proper season, which God hath determined, when he will make a resurrection of all men from the dead, not procuring a transmigration of souls from one body to another, but raising again those very bodies, which you Greeks, seeing to be dissolved, do not believe [their resurrection]: but learn not to disbelieve it;

For while you believe that the soul is created, and yet is made immortal by God, according to the doctrine of Plato, and this in time, be not incredulous; but believe that God is able, when he hath raised to life that body which was made as a compound of the same elements, to make it immortal; for it must never be said of God, that he is able to do some things, and unable to do others. We have therefore believed that the body will be raised again; for although it be dissolved, it is not perished; for the earth receives its remains, and preserves them; and while they are like *seed*, and are mixed among the more fruitful soil, they flourish, and what is *sown* is indeed sown *bare grain*;

But at the mighty sound of God the Creator, it will sprout up, and be raised in a *clothed* and *glorious* condition, though not before it has been dissolved, and mixed [with the earth]. So that we have not rashly believed the resurrection of the body; for although it be dissolved for a time on account of the original transgression, it exists still, and is cast into the earth as into a potter's furnace, in order to be formed again, not in order to rise again such as it was before, but in a state of purity, and so as never to be destroyed any more;

And to everybody shall its own soul be restored; and when it hath *clothed itself* with that body, it will not be subject to misery, but, being itself pure, it will continue with its pure body, and rejoice with it, with which it having walked righteously now in this world, and never having had it as a snare, it will receive it again with great gladness: but as for the unjust, they will receive their bodies not changed, not freed from diseases or distempers, nor made glorious, but with the same diseases wherein they died, and such as they were in their unbelief, the same shall they be when they shall be faithfully judged.

6. For all men, the just as well as the unjust, shall be brought before *God the word*; for to him hath *the Father committed all judgment*; and he in order to *fulfill the will of his Father*, shall come as judge, whom we call *Christ*. For Minos and Rhadmanthus are not the judges, as you Greeks do suppose, but he whom *God even the Father hath glorified*; **concerning whom we have elsewhere given a more particular account, for the sake of those who seek after truth**.

This person, exercising the righteous judgment of the Father towards all men, hath prepared a just sentence for everyone, according to his works; at whose judgment seat when all men, and angels, and demons shall stand, they will send forth one voice, and say, **just is thy judgment**; the rejoinder to which will bring a just sentence upon both parties, by giving justly to those that have done well an *everlasting fruition*;

But allotting to the lovers of wicked works *eternal punishment*. To these belong *the unquenchable fire*, and that without end, and a certain fiery *worm never dying*, and not destroying the body, but continuing its eruption out of the body with never-ceasing grief; neither will sleep give ease to these men, nor will the night afford them comfort; death will not free them from their punishment, nor will the interceding prayers of their kindred profit them; for the just are no longer seen by them, nor are they thought worthy of remembrance;

But the just shall remember only their righteous actions whereby they have attained *the heavenly kingdom*, in which there is no sleep, no sorrow, no corruption, no care, no night, no day measured by time, no sun driven in his course along the circle of heaven by necessity; and measuring out the bounds and conversions of the seasons, for the better illumination of the life of men; no moon decreasing and increasing, or introducing a variety of seasons, nor will she then moisten the earth; no burning sun, no Bear turning round [the pole], no Orion to rise, no wandering of innumerable stars.

The earth will not then be difficult to be passed over, nor will it be hard to find out the court of Paradise, nor will there be any fearful roaring of the sea, forbidding the passengers to walk on it: even that will be made easily passable to the just, though it will not be void of moisture.

Heaven will not then be uninhabitable by men; and it will not be impossible to discover the way of ascending thither. The earth will not be uncultivated, nor require too much labor of men, but will bring forth its fruits of its own accord, and will be well adorned with them.

There will be no more generations of wild beasts, nor will the substance of the rest of the animals shoot out any more; for it will not produce men, but the number of the righteous will continue, and never fail, together with righteous angels, and spirits [of God], and with his word, as a choir of righteous men and women that never grow old and continue in an incorruptible state, singing hymns to God, who hath advanced them to that happiness, by the means of a regular institution of life; with whom the whole creation also will lift up a perpetual hymn from *corruption to incorruption* as glorified by a splendid and pure spirit. It will not then be restrained by a bond of necessity, but with a lively freedom shall offer up a voluntary hymn, and shall praise him that made them, together with the angels, and spirits, and men now *freed from all bondage.*

7. And now, if you Gentiles will be persuaded by these motives, and leave your vain imaginations about your pedigrees, and gaining of riches and philosophy, and will not spend your time about subtilties of words, and hereby lead your minds into error, and if you will apply your ears to the hearing of the inspired prophets, the interpreters, both of God and of his word, and will believe in God, you shall both be partakers of these things, and obtain the good things that are to come, you shall see the ascent into the immense heaven plainly, and that kingdom which is there; for what God hath now concealed in silence [will be then made manifest] *what neither eye hath seen, nor ear hath heard, nor hath it entered into the heart of man the things that God hath prepared for them that love him.*

8. *In whatsoever ways I shall find you in them shall I judge you entirely;* so cries the **end** of all things. And he who hath at first lived a virtuous life, but towards the latter end falls into vice, these labors by him before endured, shall be altogether vain and unprofitable, even as in a play, brought to an ill catastrophe.

Whosoever shall have lived wickedly and luxuriously may repent; however, there will be need of much time to conquer an evil habit, and even after repentance his whole life must be guarded with great care and diligence, after the manner of a body, which, after it hath been a long time afflicted with a distemper, requires a stricter diet and method of living; for though it may be possible, perhaps, to break off the chain of our irregular affections at once, — yet our amendment cannot be secured without the grace of God, the prayers of good men, the help of the brethren, and our own sincere repentance and constant care.

It is a good thing not to sin at all; it is also good, having sinned, to repent, — as it is best to have health always; but it is a good thing to recover from a distemper. *To God be glory and dominion for ever and ever. Amen.*

CHAPTER 15

The Removal of Paradise From Hades To Heaven

I knew a man in Christ above fourteen years ago ... such an one CAUGHT UP to the third heaven. And I knew such a man ... How that he was CAUGHT UP INTO PARADISE.

- 2 Corinthians 12:2-4

Paradise is now in the third heaven. Before Christ's resurrection this wasn't the case. Paradise, also called Abraham's bosom, was located in *hades*, the abode of the dead. It wasn't until after Christ's resurrection that the righteous, when they died, went up to heaven.

We first learn of paradise's location as being in *hades/sheol* with Jacob's statement after the supposed death of his son, Joseph. Notice:

...I will go down into *sheol* unto my son mourning.
- Genesis 37:35

I realize the *King James Version* says, *"I will go down into 'the grave' unto my son mourning,"* but this is clearly an incorrect translation of the Hebrew word *sheol*. It couldn't be "the grave" Jacob was referring to here, simply because he didn't have any idea where Joseph's body was laid for him to go unto. Actually, he was under the impression by his other sons that Joseph had been devoured by wild animals. Therefore, in his thinking, Joseph's body wasn't in any grave that he could join to be with at his own death. Notice again:

I will go down into *sheol* UNTO MY SON mourning.

Thus, it wouldn't make sense for him to say, "I will go down into the grave *unto my son* mourning." Again, in his mind, there wasn't a grave Joseph's body was laid in, so he couldn't join his son in the grave. Therefore, there is no doubt that *sheol* could *not* be translated "the grave." Jacob was clearly talking about being reunited with Joseph in the afterlife, in *sheol*. Because of Joseph's supposed hideous death, Jacob would go down mourning, as would any parent who had lost a child in such a way.

There are several lessons we can learn about the afterlife from this one verse:

1) *sheol*, the abode of the dead, was not up, but *down*. Jacob said, "I will go **down** into *sheol* unto my son mourning." (See chapter 4, Where Is Hell?)

2) Jacob obviously believed in a life following his earthly life. He would go down into *sheol* **unto his son**. He

believed that he would be reunited with his son after physical death.

    3) Because we know from many, many other verses in the Old Testament that the wicked also went down into *sheol*, we again see that **both** the righteous and unrighteous went down into *sheol*.

    Thus, before Christ's resurrection, as previously brought out, the righteous and unrighteous dwelt in the same abode, yet separated by a great gulf (Luke 16:19-31). Lest there be any doubt that paradise was at one time in *sheol/hades*, we have Jesus' own words:

    ...Verily I say unto thee, today shalt thou be with me IN PARADISE.

                                          - Luke 23:43

    For as Jonah was three days and three nights in the whale's belly; so shall the Son of man be three days and three nights in the HEART OF THE EARTH.

                                    - Matthew 12:40

    ...Touch me not, for I am not yet ascended unto my Father:

                                        - John 20:17

    When Jesus was on the cross, one of the dying thieves at his side asked Jesus to remember him when He came into His kingdom. Jesus immediately responded, *"Today thou shalt be with me in paradise."* Yet three days after his death on the cross, Jesus clearly said that he hadn't yet ascended to be with his Father, *"Touch me not, for I am not yet ascended unto my Father."* If paradise had been located in heaven, Jesus would have ascended to his Father immediately upon his death on the cross. Thus, paradise was obviously located at that time somewhere other than heaven. According to his own words He was in the heart of the earth those three days and three nights.

The apostle Paul gives us further insight:

Now that he ascended, what is it but that he also descended FIRST INTO THE LOWER PARTS OF THE EARTH?

- Ephesians 4:9

Before Jesus ascended to heaven after his resurrection, he *first* descended into the lower parts of the earth upon his death for three days and three nights. Since Jesus told the thief on the cross, *"Today shalt thou be with me in paradise,"* we now have it confirmed that paradise was in the lower parts of the earth in *sheol/hades*. However, *after Christ's resurrection, that gloriously changed!* While in *sheol/hades* Jesus decisively conquered death and hell and, at his resurrection, conquered the grave. All three had no choice but to bow their knee to the Prince of Life.

I am he that liveth and was dead (the grave and spiritual separation from God)**; and, behold, I am alive forevermore, Amen; and have the keys of hell** (*hades*) **and of death.**

- Revelation 1:18

All those from Adam to Christ who served the living God were in paradise. All from Adam to Christ who did *not* serve the living God were on the other side of the great gulf in torment. Those in paradise were looking expectantly to the coming messiah. They knew the day was coming when, although they were in comfort, they would be released from the lower parts of the earth to a *heavenly* bliss. They looked forward to the gates of *hades* being opened by the One who would obtain the keys.

It would be fascinating to have some of the conversation that took place in paradise among the faithful during the 4,000 or so years they were confined. No doubt as each new generation entered they would give all of the rest whatever further information about the messiah they had been given. Family members would give other family members the latest news from the earth about their friends and loved ones. As the more well known ministers, such as Isaiah, Daniel, and Ezekiel, entered paradise they would share what God had done in the earth through their ministries, as well as add to the growing picture of the messiah to come.

Of course, when people such as Martha and Mary's brother, Lazarus, died and entered paradise, they gave first hand information about the messiah. They now knew his name was Jesus. Surely they thrilled their listeners with the incredible reports of the miraculous element in His ministry. Certainly some of the miracle type ministers of the Old Covenant, such as Elisha, thoroughly enjoyed all that they heard.

Since they were now aware that the messiah, Jesus,

was on the earth, they knew their time of confinement was drawing to a close. No doubt it was a time of great enthusiasm. Excitement was in the air amongst the inhabitants of paradise — *"What was it going to be like in heaven? What was it going to be like to see a sky again? What was it going to be like to actually be in the presence of God, to see the throne of the universe?"* It must have been a time of awesome exuberance.

As we saw from Luke chapter 16:19-31, there was occasionally conversation across the gulf between the two compartments. Certainly all of this news and excitement about the messiah moved across the gulf to the unrighteous inhabitants. Surely they had heard He was going to unlock the gates of *hades* and release all those in paradise. Sadly, they must have wished that they, too, might somehow be released from their torment, with the hopes He would release all compartments. Of course, any hopes they would have would shortly be dashed to the ground.

When Jesus died on the cross, his spirit and soul descended into *hades*. While in *hades* He obtained the keys (i.e. the authority) to *hades* and death. At some point He traveled freely back and forth between the two sections, something that had never been done before. It would be of tremendous interest, to say the least, to have seen everything that took place with Jesus during those three days and nights. Paradise must have been rejoicing, and hell must have been cursing. On the third day, according to God's timetable, it was time for His resurrection from the dead. His physical body in the tomb awaited its reuniting with the spirit and soul of Jesus.

All those in paradise were getting ready for a transportation up to heaven. The redeemed must have seemed almost giddy with anticipation. The atmosphere was charged with joy and happy delight among the millions of redeemed. That for which they had looked forward was on the verge of taking place.

Unfortunately, for the unsaved, we can almost imagine them pushing against the doors of their confinement, so to speak, with their hands on the bars and their faces peering through in hopes that they, too, might escape. Whatever hopes they had, if any, were soundly rejected as they heard the praises of the redeemed slowly fade away in the far distance as they jubilantly ascended up out of hades. When the gate slammed shut, so to speak, they fell to their knees weeping and cursing. Nothing to look forward to, only fear and dread of their final judgment, whenever that may be. Alone in their thinking, they cursed the times on earth they ignored the many promptings of the Holy Spirit.

Jesus led this multitude of thrilled inhabitants up into the third heaven. Now when the saved die, they go straight up into heaven.

I knew a man in Christ above fourteen years ago ... such an one CAUGHT UP to the third heaven. And I knew such a man ... How that he was CAUGHT UP INTO PARADISE.
- 2 Corinthians 12:2-4

It must have been a loud, almost raucous, if such a term could be used, time of praise. This was not, most assuredly, a time of quiet introspection. It was a time of victory, a time for rapturous exaltation in the singing of appreciation and adulation, a time for shouting, a time for dancing. We can imagine the wonderment in their eyes as they beheld the streets of gold, the 216 ft. high wall composed of 12 precious stones encompassing the city, the gates of pearl, and the awe-inspiring mansions that had been prepared for them.

From what we read in Psalm 150, there were surely musical instruments joining in amongst their praise. Cymbals were crashing, tambourines were shaking, stringed instruments were plucking and bowing, trumpets were blasting. Most likely, bands were playing and choirs were singing. Oohs and ahs must have been on everyone's lips — *"Look at this. Look at that. What's that over there? What kind of animal is that? Have you ever seen an angel so tall? I never dreamed this place could be so beautiful."*

The angels welcomed everyone to heaven. They explained their new surroundings, gave directions when needed, and answered questions when asked. In a sense, they must have been like heavenly tour guides. With millions of the redeemed in tow, there must have been hundreds of thousands of angels designated by God to lead everyone to their corresponding villages and homes. Possibly there is a heavenly Chinatown, a heavenly little Italy, areas where certain groups of believers might want to congregate to rejoice with family, friends, and others from their national heritage. It must have been exciting to hear the many different tongues and yet been able to understand all that was being said.

In everyone's new mansion, possibly there were new wardrobes provided in the closets; clothes made from the finest weaves, silks, and cottons; the brightest colors, fashionable and angelic styles, tailored for perfect fits. It's difficult to imagine as diverse as God is that we'll wear white robes all the time. Mansions were made of the highest quality of wood, others from outstanding marble, most from a combination of both. Whatever the heart desired, every detail was fully accounted for.

There were courtyards, gardens, walkways, and flower beds. The countryside was beautiful, the city magnificent. The lakes and streams were crystal clear, not too cold, but just the right temperature for wading or swimming. One could lie in the grass without worrying about bug bites or rashes. Children could climb trees, run, play, and explore. There was nothing in heaven that could hurt or destroy.

Heaven isn't a state of mind. It is a real, actual place. Millions of saints are presently in detailed preparation for the ages yet to come. There is activity, eternal lessons to be grasped and implemented, mysteries being revealed. Certainly angels were filling the greater number of these teaching roles until the redeemed were ready to fill these positions. At the appropriate time after the wonder had simmered down, the One who sat upon the throne addressed the multiplied millions. The majestic words that fell from the Creator's lips held the host spellbound. He made clear to them what the apostle Paul would later reveal in his letters to the churches — God was their Father and they were His children. His purpose in creating man was to have a family. God wasn't some gigantic spiritual CEO, He was truly a Father welcoming His children home.

What a time it must have been. Then, when Jesus, in all of His glory, stood in front of this considerable host of angels and saints, every knee willingly fell to the ground, every head bowed in worship, and every tongue whispered in reverence to the Lordship of their Savior. A holy silence fell throughout the massive ranks, and then, as if on cue, the silence was broken and the multiplied millions lifted their hands and their voices and sang in unison, *"Thou art worthy, O Lord, to receive glory and honor and power: for thou hast created all things, and for thy pleasure they are and were created."*

When believers die they no longer go to *hades*. That section where the righteous from Adam to Christ were contained is an empty reminder to those in torment on the other side of the great gulf. If only they had made the right decisions on earth, they wouldn't be where they presently are. As the empty tomb is a reminder to believers on earth that Jesus is alive, the empty section in *hades* is a reminder to unbelievers that the righteous are alive in bliss. The good news for us is that a Christian will never go through those gates. Jesus plainly said:

...the gates of *hades* shall not prevail against (the Church).

- Matthew 16:18

When Christians die, because of the resurrection of Jesus, they go UP into paradise.

CHAPTER 16

Paradise Is Now In Heaven

In my Father's house are many mansions: if it were not so, I would have told you. I go to prepare a place for you.

- John 14:2

We are confident, I say, and willing rather to be absent from the body, and to be present with the Lord.
- 2 Corinthians 5:8

We can only imagine the unlimited joy and happiness among the saints in heaven. It will be fascinating just to lay our eyes on the ministers of the Old and New Testaments, to actually see what Abraham looked like, or Joshua, or Isaiah, or Peter, or Barnabus. What did Noah look like? What did Moses' voice sound like? Did Paul have curly hair or straight? What kind of personalities did these people have? Were they out-going or reserved, loud or quiet, humorous or serious? Certainly there was and is a mixture of diverse personalities amongst the host of heaven.

It will be most interesting to hear their stories first hand. To hear from Noah the details about the deluge and the building of the ark. To hear from Daniel about Nebuchadnezzar, Belshazzar, and the lion's den. To listen to David and his victory over Goliath, etc. It's not hard to imagine that there will be testimonial meetings where some of the more noted personalities will share what God did for them and through them in their day. We'll rejoice over the victories and conquests God gave them while on the earth.

It will be most glorious to walk hand-in-hand with our loved ones on the streets of gold, to enjoy such a place with our husband or wife, our sons, and our daughters. To be with our parents, brothers, and sisters as we explore the different areas of paradise. Then to meet and make new friends from different parts of the world or people from different eras of earth's history. It will be most interesting to visit with people similar in personality to us who lived 3,000 years ago, or 1,500 years ago, or 800 years ago. There will be so much to see and do with no time constraints to hinder our enjoyment.

That in the AGES TO COME he might shew the exceeding riches of his grace in his kindness toward us through Christ Jesus.

- Ephesians 2:7

God is going to continually show us the vast riches of all that He has prepared for us *in the upcoming ages*. This is difficult to grasp. From Adam to this present day is approximately 6,000 years, which seems incredibly long to our finite minds. Yet 50,000 years from now we won't even have come close to beginning eternity. It's hard to fathom that in 500,000 years from now we'll still be existing, yet not just existing, but actually *living* an awesome and abundant life. Then to imagine a *million* years from now, a *billion* years from now, a *trillion* years from now, we'll still be eternally youthful while enjoying the mysteries of the universe as God unfolds His plan to us. Forever and ever isn't easy to comprehend at the present time.

Actually, going to heaven isn't the end, it's only the beginning. We're not going to stay in heaven, we'll be going back and forth to and from heaven. God has made an incredibly huge universe that needs exploring. Exactly what this will entail is unknown, but whatever God has in mind will be revealed to us as the ages come and go.

Earth life is so finite and constraining that for someone to trade their eternity for 70 or so years of sin on earth is ridiculously stupid. What is 70 years in comparison to 1,000,000,000,000,000,000 years of eternity? Eternity isn't going to be a time of mindlessly floating on clouds and strumming harps. It's going to be a time of activity, planning, building, and enterprising. A time of productivity and accomplishment. God is the ultimate big thinker, and what He has in mind is going to be grand and awesome.

There are several exciting facts about heaven that need to be pointed out.

1) Our minds won't be diminished as they are on earth.

For now we see through a glass darkly...now I know in part...

- 1 Corinthians 13:12

Our minds on earth are extremely limited. It's almost as if we're living in a fog, or as Paul said, looking through a glass darkly. At the present time we're only using 10% of our brains. This means that 90% of our potential has been robbed!!!! Imagine what man would accomplish if he were actually using 100% of his mind. This was how God originally created man to be. Adam was created with a potential that is mind boggling to us today. Fallen man is far removed from God's original plan. When man sinned in the garden of Eden, his capacity for thinking and comprehending was drastically reduced.

However, when we enter heaven we will no longer look through a glass darkly. Our spirit is already back to what God originally intended through the new birth, but our soul (the mind, will, and emotions) will be *quickened* when we enter heaven. We'll no longer be hindered by the 90% brain incapacitation which has rendered us to the 10% use we've been accustomed to. We will actually have 100% use of our thinking and potential. Our minds are a wondrous tool that will be restored to what they should have been all along.

As a result, we'll be better able to enjoy the wonders of heaven. For example, we've all seen children who were born with varying degrees of mental retardation. Incidentally, in heaven their minds, too, will be restored to their full operational capacity. But the point is, their capacity now for enjoying life is correspondingly diminished. Yes, they can smile, experience pleasure, and feel love, but the *degree* that they can fully assimilate these is on a much lower scale than someone with a higher IQ. It's interesting because the more intelligent the person, the greater the possibility for enjoying life. Paradoxically, though, is the greater the possibility for experiencing depression. This is another reason why hell will be so bad and heaven will be so good. Because the mind will be restored to its unhindered condition outside of the physical body, the enjoyments of heaven will be so much more grand. Unfortunately for the person in hell, this will also make their suffering all the worse. The greater their understanding and comprehension, the deeper their torment is felt.

Of course, for those of us who believe, heaven will be all the more wonderful. To have our spirit *and* soul functioning at its apex will open a floodgate of enjoyment that is presently unknown to us. Because of our only using 10% of our minds our capability to enjoy is degraded greatly. Though we smile, experience pleasure, and feel love, the degree that we can assimilate these is retarded in comparison to when we'll have the 100% use of our soul. We truly don't have any comprehension of love, happiness, and joy. We likewise don't have any comprehension of hate, depression, and sadness. How glorious heaven will actually be and how damning hell will actually be is difficult to fully describe. Nevertheless, our minds will be *fully* functional.

2) All tears will be wiped away.

And God shall wipe away all tears from their eyes; and there shall be no more death, neither sorrow, nor crying, neither shall there be any more pain: for the

former things are passed away.

- Revelation 21:4

This world is a world of sorrow. Devastating emotional stress and trauma is an every day part of life on earth. Whether it is our children suffering or our parents suffering, or husband, wife, brothers, sisters, or friends, we are constantly having to deal with personal loss many, many times in some form or fashion. Divorce, financial setbacks, and sickness are, unfortunately, all too common. Tears are shed again and again in trying to deal with the personal loss, pain, and heartache.

In heaven this will come to an end. *Every* tear will be wiped away. Depression, tragedy, and heartache will no longer be experienced. These are all the by-product of sin, and because sin will be totally eliminated its corresponding foul offspring will be eliminated, too. No more pain, no more sorrow, no more sickness, and no more death. Heaven will encompass all that its name suggests.

Some have asked, "How could I not have any tears if I know that one of my loved ones is in hell?" It's important to realize that God has never solved any of mankind's dilemmas by keeping us in darkness and ignorance. God solves our many problems by educating us in His Word and enlightening us with *further* information.

Obviously, at present we don't understand the full-fledged mysteries of salvation, life, death, and the world of the spirit. As brought out in the preceding point, we won't know less in heaven, we'll know more. Thus, our tears being wiped away won't be based on our lack of knowledge but rather on our completed knowledge. Evidently, God will explain to us those things that we don't fully understand now. We can rest assured that God, who does all things well, will amply satisfy our every question and longing. If He, who is love incarnate, can live with people in hell, so shall we. Surely there are aspects about eternity that we don't yet comprehend. There are some issues that are difficult to deal with now because of our present mental handicaps. Therefore, it is best to trust God and leave some of these issues in His hands. At the appropriate time God will fully explain these issues that need explaining. We will be fully content with His answers. If the scripture says that the Judge of all the earth shall do right (Genesis 18:25), we can be at peace that all will one day be accounted for, be correct, and fully explained. Yes, *all* tears will be wiped away and we'll live in peace and harmony with God, ourselves, and all others.

3) There will be no more hurting and destroying.

...shall not hurt nor destroy in all my holy mountain,
- Isaiah 65:25

In heaven there will be nothing to fear, no one to dread, no virus, bacteria, or disease to worry about, and no more death. Life on earth is pitiful at best. From the moment we're born we begin to die. Without God life is meaningless, hopeless, and unforgiving. Life on earth doesn't play fair. No one is exempt from trials and tragedy. The richest person on earth down to its poorest can't run from hurt and destruction. In one way or another it comes to all.

Earth is a blurry, unfocused picture of what God originally intended it to be. Because of Adam it is a world of sorrow and pain. Walk down any hospital corridor and you'll see anguish and suffering in most every room. Herniated discs, malfunctioning kidneys, blocked arteries, heart and lung disease, diabetes, tumors, and cancer make inroads into every family. Sadly, so many suffer endlessly not knowing a life without physical discomfort and pain. Failing eyesight, hearing, tasting, losing hair, wrinkling of skin, age spots, graying hair come to pass as the body slowly declines and eventually dies. The earth is a world under an actual, literal curse.

However, nothing of this hideous curse can enter heaven's boundaries. All sickness, disease, poverty, sorrow, pain, tragedy, and depression is off limits to heaven. Heaven is a place of joy unspeakable and full of God's glory. There are no restraints to happiness, no restraints to pleasure, and no restraints to abundance. Everything about heaven is goal-oriented, exciting, fun, and fulfilling.

It's interesting how people think that goal-setting is only a part of this life. Actually, the only thing that will change from earth to heaven will be the fact that nothing can hurt or destroy anymore. Thus, if you're an artist here you'll be an artist there. If you're a musician here you'll be a musician there. If you're an architect here you'll be an architect there. If you write literature here you'll write literature there.

Why is it that people wrongly think that God put these gifts in people only for life on earth? All scientific and artistic gifts have eternal uses and purposes. Heaven is going to have the most beautiful sculptures that were ever created. The buildings and structures in heaven will be planned by some of the greatest architectural minds ever born. Science, literature, and music will all be a part of heaven.

Imagine musicians who have had centuries to further develop and perfect their craft. Imagine the compositions, the virtuosos, the orchestras, the concerts. Imagine the literature from the minds with 100% thinking capacity. Imagine the sciences, the discoveries, the many universal mysteries being unlocked. *Every* person will have a role and function in God's eternal plan. Not one person will be left out. The difference between heaven and earth is that there won't be any defects, impurities, and sin. All abilities, talents, and gifts will be fully functional and developed as eternity unfolds.

Heaven will also be a time of r&r (rest and relaxation) as we await the resurrection of our physical bodies. Surprising to some people is the fact that we won't spend eternity as just a spirit and soul. Our physical body will one day be resurrected! It won't matter if our body had been burned up, turned to ash, and blown in the wind over an open sea, God knows where every particle lies. Miraculously, every element will come together to re-form our bodies without the flaws and defects so familiar in this present world. Our physical bodies will no longer be susceptible to sickness, disease or death.

4 Facts About Our Resurrected Body

...It is sown in corruption; it is raised in

incorruption: it is sown in dishonor; it is raised in glory: it is sown in weakness; it is raised in power: it is sown a natural body; it is raised a spiritual body...

- 1 Corinthians 15:42-44

...but we know that, when he shall appear, we shall be like him; for we shall see him as he is.

- 1 John 3:2

According to Paul, our present body is perishable, in dishonor, weak, and natural. Our resurrected body will be imperishable, glorious, powerful, and spiritual. As one preacher friend of mine says, we'll be supernaturally natural and naturally supernatural. No longer confined to this natural world we'll be able to cross back and forth between this natural realm and the spirit realm with ease. We'll truly be at home in both worlds — unlimited, imperishable, glorious, and supernatural. Man was created a spirit with a soul at home in a physical body (1 Thessalonians 5:23). All that man originally was, man will once again be. Actually, *better*.

Rewards

Just as there are degrees of judgment for those in hell, at the other end of the spectrum there are degrees of rewards for those in heaven. Of course, all sins will have been blotted out and not even remembered. If Jesus Christ is the Lord of our lives we will enter heaven. Our salvation has nothing to do with the judgment seat of Christ. The judgment seat of Christ has only to do with our *works*. Here our *works* will be judged.

Every man's WORK shall be made manifest: for the day shall declare it, because it shall be revealed by fire; and the fire shall try every man's WORK of what sort it is. If any man's WORK abide which he hath built thereupon, he shall receive a REWARD. If any man's WORK shall be burned, he shall suffer loss: but he himself shall be saved; yet as by fire.

- 1 Corinthians 3:13-15

At the appointed time all believers will stand before Christ to give an account for what they did while in the body. Were we faithful to do what *He* wanted us to do? Or did we do what *we* wanted to do? Did we give up His calling on our life because circumstances in life got difficult? Or did we stay faithful to the end through thick and thin because obeying God was more important to us?

For those who obeyed God, did they do it with the right motives? Or were they more concerned with being seen by men? For example, on one occasion concerning the giving of alms Jesus warned His disciples not to sound a trumpet to be seen of men. If they did, that would be their only reward. But if our motive is pure, simply giving a cup of cold water in the name of Christ will register a reward to our account.

Our motive for doing what we're doing is crucial. *Why* are we doing it? If what we're doing is only to be seen of men, we will lose any eternal reward. Wrong motives and imbalanced priorities are considered wood, hay, and stubble and will burn up leaving no reward. Yes, the work may have been a good work and helped many people, but the *personal motive* for our doing it is paramount in God's eyes. If the

159

motive is wrong, the work will be burned up.

If our priorities are right and our motives pure, and if what we're doing is for the glory of God, a reward will gladly be handed out. Jesus is looking to pass out many, many rewards. Further, He is looking to hand out positions of leadership in the world to come. On earth leadership is determined by natural abilities, but not so in the future age. Rank and authority will be determined by *faithfulness*. Were we faithful on earth to fulfill *His* plan? Did we *finish* our God-given course?

Unfortunately, many people start out sincere with great promise, but if hardship, misunderstanding, or persecution arises they falter and back off from God's plan. Others get spiritually lazy and become worldly. They still want to go to heaven, but the cares of this life slowly erode their spiritual lives. Instead of looking for friendship and support in the Church, they would rather build a network of support that backs their own plan instead of God's plan. *It's not how we begin that determines our reward, it's how we end.*

In the parable of the talents we see that promotion is based on faithfulness. One man doubled his five talents to ten and another doubled his two talents to four. When their lord returned he responded to both with the same reply:

...Well done, good and FAITHFUL servant; thou has been FAITHFUL over a few things, I WILL MAKE THEE RULER OVER MANY THINGS: enter thou into

the joy of the Lord.

- Matthew 25:21,23

What we do with what was given us and our motive for completing it is the determining factor for rulership in the age to come. Many unknown people in this age will be in high places of leadership in the next. The next age for all believers is going to be extremely exciting, *yet for some because of their faithfulness will be able to share in the leadership councils with the Lord Himself.* It will be most glorious to personally confer and receive instruction from Christ on accomplishing leadership goals throughout the future ages. As the apostle Paul said, *"...this one thing I do, forgetting those things which are behind, and reaching forth unto those things which are before. I press toward the mark for the PRIZE of the high calling of God in Christ Jesus"* (Philippians 3:13-14). Life in paradise and throughout future ages is going to be action packed and rewarding. How tragic that so many people will foolishly miss heaven and end up in hell.

CONCLUSION

I call heaven and earth to record this day against you, that I have set before you LIFE and DEATH, blessing and cursing: therefore CHOOSE LIFE, that both thou and thy seed may live:
- Deuteronomy 30: 19

I remember a number of years ago reading about some high school students who had, as a supposed prank, removed a number of stop signs at many dangerous intersections in their community. Because there were no warnings, when the unsuspecting motorists came to the intersections there were a number of serious collisions as the vehicles came at full speed from many different directions. Sadly, there were fatalities involved. The community was rightly in an uproar over what to do. People actually died because of the horrible conduct of those students.

Clearly, we need signs to help and warn us. Without appropriate warnings innocent people may die. Those who live in the Midwest recognize the importance of a failproof weather warning system because of the threat of tornados. Those who live on the coast recognize the need for warnings concerning the riptide. Pilots need air traffic controllers. The sleeping need fire alarms. If people get in a furor over physical death, how much more should we be concerned over spiritual death.

Hell is very real. The misinformed need to be warned. The uninformed need to be warned. Those who have heard but haven't received Jesus need to be warned again. Then again. And again after that. The casualty rate for those going to hell is too high. As Jesus said, the harvest is great but the laborers are few. The world needs more people sounding the alarm. Not one person has to go to hell, yet regrettably, every single day multiplied hundreds of thousands of people die and go to hell. This shouldn't be simply because the ransom was paid in the death, burial, and resurrection of Jesus.

The love of God is the most powerful of all in the created universe. Sadly, too many trifle with the love of God and spurn His love. I don't think the world realizes what a tremendous sacrifice God made to redeem mankind when He gave up His very own Son, Jesus. The truth is, when Adam and Eve fell, God didn't have to do anything for mankind. He had made the instructions very plain and simple to them. They both had been taught that if they ate of the forbidden tree they would die. Yet they willingly disobeyed God and ate of the tree. As a result, their spiritual life died that day and they became spiritually dead unto God. Their inward nature is the cause of their hell. The location of hell would only be a container for those in that same spiritual condition.

To again use the diseased/healthy analogy, we could say that the world is diseased in desperate need of healing. Jesus then opened a health clinic called Calvary to bring healing to the diseased. Yet if the diseased refuse healing they must be quarantined. For one to be quarantined it doesn't mean they are hated by the doctors, it is only a necessity that they be separated from the healthy. It is unhealthy for the diseased and healthy to intermingle. Similarly, the righteous and unrighteous cannot intermingle in the world of the spirit. Thus, hell is a spiritual quarantine. God doesn't hate the sinner, but for the sanity and well being of the universe the unrighteous must be separated from the righteous.

We have learned then that the inward nature of the unredeemed is wanton spiritual death. They cannot go to heaven because their nature is in complete disarray and out of tune with heaven. When the unredeemed die their spirit and soul leaves the physical body and begins to fully manifest its abhorrent nature. Their spiritual condition outside the body is one of intolerable pain. Spiritual suffering is far beyond physical suffering. What we witness in certain wards of hospitals concerning physical suffering, as horrendous as it is, is pale in comparison.

This is where the love of God came in. God didn't want mankind to remain in that gross spiritual condition. By any kind of law, He could have, *but God truly loves each and every person.* Therefore Jesus came to earth and willingly bore the cause of mankind's problem on Himself. This is why it is so unnecessary for anyone to go to hell. It is truly absurd. Hell shouldn't be any kind of a problem — for *man*, that is. God truly eliminated the spiritual condition and location for mankind. All mankind has to do is make the right decision.

If man wants to go to heaven the sin problem has been taken care of by Jesus. All he has to do is choose Jesus. If man doesn't want to have anything to do with God, that, too, is his decision. Basically, heaven or hell is a choice. God has presented both sides and it is up to man to choose. To use a sports analogy, we could say the ball is in our court. Whatever happens in our spiritual lives is up to us. If we go to hell we can't blame God and we can't blame any person on earth. *We have only ourselves to blame.*

I'll never forget an incident that took place in front of my eyes several years ago. As I was driving home from the airport I was in a long procession of cars likewise going home. After a prolonged length of time behind the steering wheel I was quite weary and was, more or less, blankly staring at the bumper of the car in front of me. Suddenly, without any warning, another car pulled out right in front of the car ahead of me. The driver ahead of me slammed his brakes to avoid hitting the car but to no avail. The collision was deafening. At full highway speed the two cars interlocked and rammed into a ditch. I immediately swerved to miss the two vehicles and, fortunately for me, narrowly missed them. After braking I ran to the side of the road to see if both drivers survived. Sadly, one of the car's occupants was dead. Eventually, an ambulance arrived and took the body to the hospital which, in turn, delivered it to the morgue.

The thoughts in my mind were racing, *"That driver could have been me. Because I was tired I wasn't alert. If that other car had pulled in front of me I wouldn't have been able to react quickly enough to have averted the wreck. Just like him my life as I know it could have suddenly come to an end."* At least, thankfully, because of Jesus being my Lord, I knew where I would have gone.

Conclusion

But what about *him*? Had *he* ever received Jesus as his savior? Was Jesus Christ the Lord of his life? Had he ever had a personal relationship with Jesus that transcended just going to church on holidays? If he had, the very moment he died he stepped outside of his body and began to ascend up to the third heaven. The angels of God met him in the transition and escorted him into the beauties of paradise. Perhaps he was taken straight to his mansion, or maybe to meet past loved ones, or possibly to meet the Lord Himself. Whatever he was doing, he was filled with awe and wonder.

If he hadn't received Jesus, I shuddered to think what he was experiencing at that moment. While I was staring at the wrecked cars from the side of the road he was slipping out of his physical body and beginning a downward journey into the lower parts of the earth from which he would never see the light of the sun again. It was odd envisioning where he was and what he was doing.

It Is Your Decision

Now the question rests on your shoulders. When you die where will *you* go? Is heaven in *your* future, or is hell? Is blessing in your eternity, or is cursing? No one can make you do anything but you. I encourage you to stop putting off life's greatest decision. This is more important than your retirement, or your stocks, or your employment, or your house, or your friends. Every issue of earthly life is secondary compared to your eternity. You have no guarantee you'll have time to make everything right with God before you die. Like the driver in the car ahead of me, he had no inkling 10 seconds previous to his death that he was going to die. He was probably only thinking about what he was going to eat for dinner when he got home. There was no warning when death came. His heaven or hell had already been decided. Likewise, when death comes to you your heaven or hell will have already been decided.

Make the right decision *and do it now*. It is as simple as a prayer. On the last page of this book is a prayer that you can pray. You don't have to go to church to pray it. You don't have to wait for a minister to pray it with you. You don't have to wait until you become a perfect person to pray it. God loves you just as you are. God will gladly receive you if you're good or bad, if you're sick or well, and if you're poor or rich.

Don't make the mistake those in hell made and delay your decision. There is no need to postpone something that is only in your best interest. Heaven should be in your future not hell. If you should desire it, salvation is only one prayer away.

NOTES

NOTES

NOTES

NOTES

NOTES

NOTES

NOTES

A Sinner's Prayer
To Receive Jesus As Savior

Dear Heavenly Father,

I come to you in the name of Jesus. Your Word says, *"...him that cometh to me I will in no wise cast out"* (John 6:37), so I know that you won't refuse me. I thank you for that.

You also said in your Word, *"Whosoever shall call upon the name of the Lord shall be saved"* (Romans 10:13), so I am calling on your name. I now believe you have saved me!

You said, *"if thou shalt confess with thy mouth the Lord Jesus, and shalt believe in thine heart that God hath raised him from the dead, thou shalt be saved. For with the heart man believeth unto righteousness; and with the mouth confession is made unto salvation"* (Romans 10:9-10).

I believe in my heart that Jesus Christ is the Son of God. I believe that He was raised from the dead for my salvation. I now confess Jesus as my Lord. I have now become the righteousness of God in Christ (2 Corinthians 5:21). I am saved. Thank you, Lord!

In Jesus' name I pray, Amen.

Signed_____

Date_____